C0-AMS-336

Art: an everyday experience

N
7430
W 3.4

Art: an everyday experience

Esther S. Warner

HARPER & ROW, PUBLISHERS, NEW YORK, EVANSTON, AND

LONDON

GOSHEN COLLEGE LIBRARY
GOSHEN, INDIANA

ART: AN EVERYDAY EXPERIENCE

Copyright © 1963 by Esther S. Warner

Printed in the United States of America. All rights reserved. No part of this book may be used or reproduced in any manner whatsoever without written permission except in the case of brief quotations embodied in critical articles and reviews. For information address Harper & Row, Publishers, Incorporated, 49 East 33rd Street, New York 16, N. Y.

LIBRARY OF CONGRESS CATALOG CARD NUMBER: 63–7668

THIS BOOK IS FOR JO DENDEL, MY HUSBAND,

WHO IS MORE THAN HALF OF ALL I AM OR DO.

Contents

PREFACE   *ix*

I   Thought patterns for art and living

1   FOREWORD: A PHILOSOPHY   5
2   AN AFRICAN FABLE: THE BEGINNING OF WISDOM   *12*
3   WAYS OF DOING   *16*
4   THE ART OF EMPATHY   *22*
    The element of line   Balance   Other empathic responses
5   AWARENESS THROUGH WORK   *30*
    Awareness of natural forms

II   The arts of making

6   SUBJECTIVE APPROACHES TO DESIGN   *45*
    Collage   Encaustic   Subjective use of a compass   Play

vii

*with negative shapes   The scribble   Leadings from
the tool   Line over mass   Haiku and other intuitive
approaches to design*

7   OBJECTIVE APPROACHES TO DESIGN   82
*That's why rulers are made   Fractures: the subdivisions of
space   Dark corner to dark corner approach   Design
through following structure of poetry forms   Repetition
with variation   Design through limitation   Design with
stick figures   Manipulation of the plastic elements of
design*

8   THE ART OF GROUP-DOING   148

III   The art of choosing and arranging

9   THE ART OF CHOOSING   157
*Escape from the ordinary   The foundations of taste
Creative collecting*

10 THE ART OF ARRANGING   170
*Composition   Architecture as composition in space   Fur-
nishings as composition within space   Composition in two
dimensions   The art of making a garden   A meal is a
composed ritual*

11 JUDGMENTS: HOW SHALL WE KNOW WHAT WE HAVE
    WROUGHT?   205
Unity   Rhythm   Balance   Proportion   Dominance

12 CONCLUSION: EASTER EGG HUNT IN SERENDIP   218

INDEX   223

Preface

Each man must seek for himself the people who hold the eternal beauty, and each man must eventually say to himself as I do, "these are my people and all that I have I owe to them". *

Robert Henri

"My people," used in the sense Robert Henri used the phrase, are multitude. Each of them is somehow in this book. They include my hosts and companions during the time I spent in tribal African villages. They include my hundreds of students at Orange Coast College and at Denwar Studio. With them I grow and learn through our joint-doing. My teachers are represented in number, particularly, Miss Edna O'Bryan and Miss Mabel Fisher of Iowa State University, and Dr. Pearl Hogrefe of

---

* Robert Henri, *The Art Spirit,* compiled by Margery Ryerson, Philadelphia and New York, Lippincott, 1951.

the same school, who interested me in writing as an art expression. "My people" also include Harriet and Vetta Goldstein, authors of *Art in Everyday Life,* whose companionship and encouragement has been a continuing inspiration since I taught in their department at the University of Minnesota.

Particular thanks are due Miss Marjorie Garfield, head of the Applied Art Department of the College of Home Economics of Iowa State University and Miss Mary Jane Haden, Consultant in Art Education, Orange County, California.

Miss Jean Stange, Assistant Professor in the Department of Textiles, Clothing and Related Art in the College of Home Economics of Michigan State University has been untiring in her enthusiastic help in preparing material for photography, and in other ways too numerous to mention.

My parents, Mr. and Mrs. Lewis Sietmann of Laurel, Iowa, are particularly "my people" in that they continually fostered that "art spirit" of which Robert Henri writes so movingly.

The interest of the two hard-working photographers, Mr. Arlie Toulouse and Mr. Lee Payne, who took most of the pictures for this book, amounts to a collaboration.

E. S. W.

I *Thought patterns for art and living*

1 Foreword: a philosophy

The purpose of this book is ambitious. That purpose is to help you become intensely alive through artistic activity. Activity means doing something. When art comes to life in your life, it is as Gerard Manley Hopkins said of peace,

> . . . and when Peace here does house
> He comes with work to do, he does not come to coo, . . .[1]

There has, I think, been too much cooing about art and too little doing. I want to nudge you, perhaps even provoke you into making design a joyful and everyday adventure. We need a rapture, or, not being able to rise to rapture, an excitement, or perhaps not being able to raise any excitement at first, then an interest, even an excited interest in what is daily and in what is often weary. Art has within it the power to make something out of the ordinary from the ordinary.

[1] Gerard Manley Hopkins, "Peace," in *The Atlantic Book of British and American Poetry*, edited by Dame Edith Sitwell, Boston, Little Brown, 1958.

When this becomes characteristic and not just a once-in-a-while fringe benefit, we have come alive through art. This is part of what Franz Kafka was trying to tell us, I believe, when he wrote a story called "Josephine the Singer or the Mouse Folk." Josephine made a "ceremonial performance out of doing the usual thing."[2]

You have a right to ask me what would be the good of making a ceremonial performance out of, say, washing the dishes. I can wash dishes without thinking, and so can you. This is precisely the glory of dishwashing. It releases me to muse and dream. I can think about anything I wish to think about. If my thoughts are delighting me, that makes the ceremony. I can wash dishes without involving all of my faculties in the process; what is not engaged is free to have full play elsewhere. I can prop a book up on the window ledge and memorize a poem. Or I can watch the soap bubbles rise and float and break and see in them the pattern of my next mosaic. I can be vacuuming the rug, and while I am doing this with reasonable efficiency, I can observe how the rain runs down the window pane and how the wind catches these rivulets and sweeps them across the glass, counter to the downward pull of gravity. Without neglecting the rug too much, I can memorize this pattern. It may come out, as it did for one of our Student Fellowship, in a blue and green stitchery which will preserve the pleasure of cool rain trickles long after our California hills have turned dry. When I have to attend to the work at hand to avoid the legs of furniture, I can see, if I am up to this, a hundred patterns in the way the brush on the vacuum lifts and leaves the loops of the rug. It is interesting to me to vacuum the rug because all the little accidental images made by the beater will never happen just that way again. If I do not attend to them, I have missed something I will not be permitted to see again in exactly the same way. While I watched the rain on the pane and was delighted by that, I missed something happening in the rug. I know that I did. We have it in our ability to make creative vision erase the routine in daily chores.

I know, too, that there have been days when everything has seemed too ordinary to bear. Daytime was a long empty yawn, and night was an endless tedium of restless wakefulness. When we had scurried through the chores of the day, not bothering about the patterns in the

2 *Selected Stories of Franz Kafka,* New York, Random House (The Modern Library), 1952.

rug (we are not always alive enough for that), it had been through dark mole-runs where the light of joy did not reach. When night came the darkness was not welcome. Indeed we had been in darkness throughout the day which should have been bright. There was no grandeur or delight or play in any task.

But there have been days of another sort; days when the smallest events were significant and interesting. This was the ceremony in them.

I saw a caterpillar today and traced its feeding pattern on a leaf. I cannot tell you why there was plenitude in this experience. True, there was splendor in the color of that obstinate length of methodical fuzz. The pattern he made was unusual and exciting. But there is more to be said than that. I think I was happy because I gave my concentrated attention to a common thing.

Yesterday was less alive than today. I can recall that yesterday I would have been unwilling to invest my undivided interest in however many caterpillars there may have been working purposefully in some secret order of their own. I have now inched myself forward in a progress that must be as purposeful as the caterpillar's own. I know with absolute conviction that to design, to choose, to arrange, to make, to create, to participate, to penetrate life, even though not much deeper than today while I watched a caterpillar pattern a leaf, is how I must seek to be alive.

But, you might now argue, the talent for all this is something other people have. Most people are convinced that artists are people with some rare talent and that art is an activity for these special few rather than an integral part of all worthwhile living.

People say, "Why should I choose my own furnishings when I can hire a decorator to do it correctly? I don't trust my own taste." Or, "Why should I fumble around trying to design something original when experts, people with talent, can do it better?"

A good decorator *can* assemble furnishings which seem to belong together, but only an exceptional decorator can choose furnishings which relate in a personal way to the people who will use them. If what we own does not awake some personal response in us, we really do not "have" that thing. It is just there, around, unfelt, not doing anything good to you or for you. If, when you dust, you resent having to flick the dust rag over a certain object, you'd better get rid of that object. It is burdening your life, not contributing to it. We need to apprehend our

7

possessions. When one is surrounded by objects to which he does not respond, the setting is wrong no matter how "correct" it is.

As for making an original arrangement (a design), the important thing is not the design but rather what doing an original design will do for you.

I cannot reveal to you how to become an artist. Nor can any teacher. Art is only partly a matter of learning with one's head. Mostly it is a way of feeling, a way of responding which leads one to ways of doing. This is not a book of assertions, not a packaged kit of rules. It is not a book to tell you what to believe or do in order to have "good taste." The goal of this book and of all my teaching is to provide a few approaches toward reviving imagination and directing it into joyful activity. I want your private world to brim with meaning. I want art to give nobility to daily living. I want you to discover your own buried resources. I want you to find satisfaction and refreshment for the spirit in art activity. I want us to become a nation of emotionally solvent souls with inner strength to sustain the assaults being made upon the spiritual values of our long inheritance. Each one of us needs to make his own good fight against the aridity of life.

"My happiness is made of fervor." André Gide says this in many ways in his *Fruits of the Earth*.[3] How does one go about learning fervor? It matters not whether your intention is to build a house, to write a novel, to weave a place mat or to find a friendship, you can not achieve one of these things with any sort of success unless it is a thing you deeply desire to do. Response is the first demand of aliveness.

The beginning, then, is to gain a purpose in living. It means getting off the bank and into the stream. It means getting involved. It means doing things with every sense alert and contributing and responding. If nothing is interesting to you at the moment, try involving yourself in a searching inquiry of a seed pod, a searching inquiry of anything. Afterwards you will realize that the moments brightened in exact proportion to the concentration of your inquiry. No one else can give you a valid aesthetic experience. Your own senses can if you allow this to happen. Joy is brought into living when all the faculties are participant in ordinary affairs.

André Kostelanetz tells about visiting Matisse in 1945 and asking him, "What is your inspiration?" The reply, "I grow artichokes." Then

[3] André Gide, *Fruits of the Earth,* New York, Alfred A. Knopf, 1949.

the explanation, "They inspire me. Every morning I go into the garden and watch the plants. I see the play of light and shadow on the leaves."[4]

We begin then, I believe, by desiring to begin and by involving our senses in the small daily dramas about us. We focus attention, we sharpen our vision, we increase consciousness. We assemble materials. We are ready to experiment in a spirit of play and adventure. We desire an enterprise of the spirit. We are going to try not to be self-conscious about this; we are not going to worry about whether what we create is or is not "art."

What follow in this book are some suggestions for experiments with materials and choices. They are offered in the sincere belief that the amount of talent one thinks he does or does not possess is of no matter. What is important is the delight that comes from using whatever ability one does possess to the fullest. This does not mean that we are going to start free-wheeling through a stack of art supplies and call everything we come up with a work of art. Let's call them investigations.

Perhaps you are willing to go along with this (although those who incline to set rules and those who prefer safety to adventure will not be willing). You are willing, you really want to design and choose and arrange, but you simply do not know how to start. We will talk about that.

Let me tell you about a highly creative, hard-working group in Orange County, California, which we call a Student Fellowship. Some of the members are established artists. Most of them are rather recent beginners. I am the instructor, but when I am doing my best as an instructor, I am the most ardent student. Each of us is the beneficiary of the investigations of everyone.

Some of the design devices with which we work are old ones which we have inherited from designers who worked far away and long ago. Some are of recent innovation. These approaches are the vehicles which carry our attempts to say something worth saying in an uniquely personal way. We do not try to be different just to be different. Each of us tries to be unique because each of us *is* unique. If compositions which start from the same design approach come out looking alike, it is agreed that we have failed. Either we had nothing to say, no feeling for what we were doing, or else we were unable to get what we did feel into the

[4] *This I Believe,* foreword by Edward R. Murrow, New York, Simon and Schuster, 1952.

9

statement we tried to make. If an art effort fails, if it lacks a fresh, unseen-before appearance, it is probably because the student did not relate all the riches of his accumulated life experience to the work or because he had insufficient technique to state what he felt.

Here we have a double-edged sword. There are artists whose technique is flawless but whose work is sterile. They know how to tell but have nothing to say to us. I prefer to spend my life sharpening the other side of the blade, working with those who have a passionate desire, a burning urgency to come alive through art expression, but who may fumble about a bit in their efforts to express. I find the evidences of a fumbling, honest struggle an endearing part of an art effort and much more compelling than the virtuoso exhibitions of the "slick" and over-clever.

Our Fellowship has investigated all of the approaches detailed in this book, and they have pooled the findings. We have held impassioned discussions which last over coffee until the small hours. When we finally went home, usually it was not to sleep, but to experiment while a new idea had us in its grasp.

The purpose of this book, then, is to provide you with a few tools which we have found useful in prying open doors to release the artist which was born in each of us. I travel with you, not as an "expert" or as a critic but as a sort of accomplice in activities which have as their consequence a resourceful personal life in which you will be interesting to yourself.

Each of us has an obligation to himself to get some enjoyment out of his own thoughts. Art is one of the few remaining areas where man can be director and doer and dreamer, all at one and the same time. It is the way to intensify the moment.

No one in our Fellowship would lay claim to having produced great art, even though a satisfying number of national and international recognitions have come to our members. What any of us would lay honest claim to is personal creative growth without which life would not be living.

We are prone to consider ourselves amateurs. The word *amateur* comes from the latin word *amore,* to love! If you question this, look it up in an unabridged dictionary. By common usage, however, the word has come to mean a dabbler. Most often it is said in disparagement. We do not love every experiment we try, but we love trying it. We do not always love what we have done, but we love doing it. We do not down-grade competence, but we do exalt compulsion. We love the feeling of the needing to express the unique, individual self and believe that this feeling is indeed, the beginning of wisdom.

2 An African fable:
the beginning of wisdom

The beginning of wisdom, says a West African proverb, *is to get you a roof.*

Here is the West African folk tale from which the proverb is taken:

When Maker had finished fashioning the first man out of a scrap of clay, Maker set man down on the crest of a rainbow and gave him a small push which sent him sliding down to earth over smooth, fire-bright color through thread-soft rain. When man finished this grand slide through the sky, he stood upright and looked upon the new earth to which he had come. Man felt fear. He looked back up the bright band of color and longed to return to

Maker. The long curve of the rainbow was slick and steep. There were no hand-holds to help the climb. Man made a few determined tries. He could not rise one step. There was no return.

Man turned his back on the sky-bow and sat down with his head in his hands. His body shivered in the rain. His heart was cold. Man was lonely. Lonely is cold.

Maker, standing at the top of the rainbow, looked down on the shivering loneliness below and was sad. "I should not have sent man down there," Maker thought. "But it is done. Well, at least, I'll send down after him a packet of Sense. That will help a little."

Maker wrapped Sense in a scrap of cloud and sent it down the rainbow after miserable man. The packet hit man in the middle of the back with a thump.

Man jumped to his feet and clutched Sense to his heart. The Sense in the packet was this:

"All the good in the world is home-spawned. The bad in the world can not find you under a roof of your own. Go, now! Get you a house."

Man pulled the cloud-wrapping from the Sense packet around his shoulders and had his first length of cloth. He began walking over the earth to which he had come, wondering how to get him a house. Rain-soaked mud oozed between his toes. The mud weighted his feet. He stepped up to a patch of moss on higher ground and raked at the mud with a fallen stick. When he cleaned the twig with his hands, he saw that the shape of his hand stayed in the clay, that the clay took form from his strength.

"Of these things you can make you a house," Sense told him. "Of sticks and this mud that stays on the stick and takes shape from the strength in your hands, of these you can make you a house."

When the house was built of a circle of sticks with mud forced between them, and only a door-hole was open, man went inside. He felt he had grown. He had a larger feel than when he had huddled at the foot of the sky-bow. But even with walls, he shivered because the house had no roof and the rain continued to fall.

Man looked up and saw fronds of palm trees above his head. He saw that the rain was stopped where the leaves were thick, that at the center of the tree the trunk was dry.

"Bring many leaves close together," Sense whispered. "Then you will be dry and warm."

Man roofed his house with palm thatch and saw that he had done a fine thing. He felt large; he felt warm. He was not so lonely now because lonely is cold. He was not so small now, because large is the feeling from making, from making the earth take form from the strength in the hands.

Man was hungry when this much work was done and went out of his house to find himself food. He came to a pool and saw that fish swam there with the colors of the sky-bow on their backs.

"I will have fish," man thought, and reached for them with his hands. Man fell in the pool and "lacked small" to drown. Swim-knowing was not part of the Sense packet wrapped in torn cloud. Man could have died then and never have slept in his new house except that a turtle saw him sinking and showed him what he must do to swim.

"I thank you plenty," man said when he was safe. "What, now, can I do for you?"

"Throw me a scrap of Sense, I beg you," Turtle said. "Maker never gave me a packet of Sense."

Man told turtle how he must build him a house and have a roof of his own where the bad of the world cannot reach.

Man, knowing how to swim now, caught fish while Turtle built a roof over his back. When Turtle was finished, Man saw that Turtle had done a one-more-again thing. There was pattern over the whole! Man took pleasure in what Turtle had done.

"How will I pattern my house?" Man thought about this all the way home.

When Man stood before his own walls and once again cleaned the mud from his feet with a stick, the thing he might do became a knowing in his hand. He was tired but he could not rest until he had made a pattern, much like Turtle's, by scratching his walls with the stick.

"I am clothed with a cloud, I am fed by a fish, I am roofed by leaves, and now I will take rest," Man thought. He stretched out on the floor of his house and listened to the rain drum on his roof. The sound was good. He wished Turtle had come home with him so they could listen together to the good sound that rain makes on a roof. He thought over his first day on earth. "A sky-bow is not a hand thing," Man thought. "A stick is a hand-thing." With the damp stick clutched in his fist to give comfort, he slept.

Food, clothing, shelter, were necessities but so was the "one-more-again thing!" Man's house became home with that. It was not an extra. It was not "art." It was a need. It had to be done before Man could take rest.

So it has been in all the years since. The need in first man is a first-need in us all. Sometimes buried, but somewhere inside, is that urge to find hand-holds on a tool and take pleasure in a pattern that forms under the strength in our hands.

3 Ways of doing

The first time I heard the story of the beginning of wisdom, I was living for a while in a village in the interior of Liberia, four days' walk from the coast. Before I moved into the thatched house which the chief gave me for my use, the earth floor was swept with a twig broom, the dust was settled by water flung from the fingers much as clothing is sprinkled before ironing. Grass mats so new they gave out the perfume of green growth were spread out like rugs. There was great dignity in these common earth things.

I had everything I needed in this temporary home, even time to think. My excuse for this trip through the jungle was that I wished to collect masks, folk-tales, and the handicrafts of the tribespeople. But my reason for the trip was deeper and more philosophical. There were empty spaces in my life that I wanted to fill with meanings. It seemed probable that among these hospitable people who seemed to live so completely in each passing moment I might find out something about the art of living of which the arts of doing are only a part.

I was drawn most of all to the craftsmen. The carver who told me the story of the first man gave me a wooden turtle he had made for his own house (Fig. 2). The turtle shape has been reduced to its basic geometry. The incised pattern of lines into which white clay has been rubbed is not a copy of a turtle's shell pattern, but one of the carver's fancy. I remembered Sir Herbert Read's definition of a work of art, "pattern informed by sensibility."[1] I would have known, even if I had not studied Sir Herbert, that the object in my hands was at least a minor work of art.

If I had tried to say this to the African carver, he certainly would not have known what I meant, even though he had been at the coast where

FIG. 2. *Turtle*, wood carving, anonymous African craftsman. Photo by Arlie Toulouse.

[1] Herbert Read, *The Meaning of Art*, London, Faber and Faber, 1946.

he had learned enough English to discuss a range of ideas. There is no word in his language or in his thinking which can be translated into "art." The closest one can come to it is a word which means "to make" or "to make fine." Neither Greece nor Egypt had a word for "art" and the people of the Middle Ages were unaware of what we mean when we use the word.

The truth is that although we have the word, we also have a great deal of confusion amongst us about what we mean when we use the word. "I don't know anything about art but I know what I like." That sentence has become so worn with usage that one can finish the sentence for anyone who begins it. Sometimes the words are said wistfully, sometimes with defiance.

Why is it that peoples who had no word for art were able to produce the pyramids, the Parthenon, the Gothic cathedrals, the bronzes of Benin? And we who have the word are for the most part so divorced from the creative process that many seem to brag of the alienation, even when the pain of the separation betrays itself in the eyes and the voice of the speaker?

Wide and deep is the gulf between the phrase "to make fine" and those two unfortunately-coupled words, "fine arts." It is interesting to take a quick backward look into history to see how the fissure happened. It began in the Renaissance but eroded deeply during the Industrial Revolution.

We read of Michelangelo working alone in the Sistine Chapel. We envision him working on, say, *The Last Judgment,* a fresco forty feet wide by forty-five feet high, executing the whole project himself with no assistance except for a man to grind his color. We can imagine him in a state of concern over the quality of the damp lime he used. He was artisan as well as artist. Probably, the duality of his role never entered his mind. It is we, who are all too aware of the regrettable distinction between the arts and the crafts, who think it strange that the great Michelangelo plastered the areas he painted, preparing the area for each day's painting with loving care.

After the Industrial Revolution had swept Europe, craftsmanship seemed a lost cause, and art took to the ivory tower or to bohemian seclusions. Art became a specialized self-conscious activity surrounded by an odor of sanctity. Split from craftsmanship, it became the province of a special few instead of a vital part of everyday living.

There were men who rebelled against this state of things, William Morris among them. The story of his life reads like a fiction. We admire the courage of Morris' protest against commercialism; we admire his ideal of producing beauty by hand work; we are astonished by the variety of what he produced—stained glass, wallpaper, furniture, embroidery, printing type. But we know that, in his time, the cause he fought was lost. The gears were turning. The machines were winning.

William Morris died in 1896. The turning gears have since accelerated. Such quantities of goods have been produced that it seems we have more than we need or even want. For twenty-eight weeks during 1958 and 1959 Galbraith's book, *The Affluent Society,*[2] was on the best-seller list. This book deals with the economics of our age of opulence. Professor Galbraith points out that whereas "in a country that was being carved from the wilderness, thrift and labor were the obligation of everyone," in our present state of affluence "the idle man may still be an enemy to himself. But it is hard to say that the loss of his effort is damaging society."

We are, it seems, being threatened with leisure. The loss of a man's efforts to produce consumer goods may not be damaging to society but the ways he will use his new leisure could be damaging in the extreme. Perhaps it is not the idle hands as much as the unoccupied imagination and the empty heart that is the danger. There is a feeling in most of us that life could mean more and be more than it is. There is a longing and an immense need for an unnamed something to irradiate our lives. We have learned that a plenitude of goods does not ensure an excellency of spirit.

More and more people are expressing a desire to make something, to create and pattern form. The African's desire to make things take shape from the strength in his hand is a universal need. But many are frustrated because they do not know what kind of impression to make or fear they will make a bad one. Many who know the yearning are held back from the creative venture by feelings of inadequacy or by an anxiety about whether they are capable of producing "art." Perhaps it would be well to forget for a while that we have that word in our language. This is not to say that we renounce the age-old art principles but rather to suggest that we start by getting involved in a creative activity, investing in it all our enthusiasm, applying all the sensibility

[2] Kenneth Galbraith, *The Affluent Society,* Boston, Houghton, Mifflin, 1958.

of which we are capable, and leaving ourselves open in judgment about the results.

There is evidence in every county fair in the land of the desire to manipulate material and make it take form. Usually an enormous and depressing array of articles are grouped in a department labeled "domestic arts." Inside the building are quilts and crocheted bedspreads in highly predictable patterns and such misapplications of effort as dishtowels embroidered with laughing carrots or coy, winking potatoes, and pillow cases abristle with french knots. There may even be a sequined feather duster or a fly swatter embroidered in wool yarn. We come away depressed. We have seen the end products of much doing but the doing has been mechanical, not creative, and for the most part in bad taste.

The Index of American Design points out that as early as 1830 there appeared in the United States "Berlin work," a "commercial embroidery which offered wool yarns in a selection of brilliant colors to be used with ready-made patterns already stamped on the cloth for cross-stitching."[3]

This "kit" kind of thing, with variations, expanded from cross-stitch to almost every art medium. Kits usually are sold at "hobby shops." The purchaser assembles what another has planned; he may do a "painting" by following numbers or execute a mosaic according to a ready-made pattern. Even the toys for children are joyless. There is no room left for invention. There is nothing for the purchaser to do but follow the directions on the package. The process is as mechanical as stirring up a cake mix or opening a tin can with a can opener.

Granting that the contents of a kit may be good design—although more often they are not—the score against them is that they are time-killers, or at best time-fillers. They do nothing to arouse or satisfy creative imagination which is the stuff of vital living.

How then shall we satisfy our need to invent honest, personal idioms of expression, and how can we know whether we have "informed them with sensibility"? We want to make, we want to "make fine." We are willing to undergo the anxiety which often accompanies the beginnings of invention. But how to go about it?

Plainly, there are two ways of doing. One is the mechanical, uninventive following of packaged-kits or sets of rules. The other way is alive,

[3] Erwin O. Christensen, *The Index of American Design*, New York, Macmillan, 1950, p. 103.

responsive, original doing. [People who copy what others have done or what others think are doomed to the mediocre. The way to make strong, original statements is to explore what is unique in yourself and what is to be seen in your environment. To do this we need to cultivate *empathy*. Empathy is the imaginative projection of one's own consciousness; it is identifying yourself with people and things.]

4 The art of empathy

"What I want is a hat," said the old African chief.

I had asked him what I might do for him in thanks for his having given me a house and food during my stay in his village.

"But you have a hat," I pointed out. "And it is new."

He was wearing a black velvet pill-box embroidered in geometric pattern with vivid yarns. It was the kind of close-fitting skull cap brought south from French territory by the Mandingo traders.

"This on my head," said the chief, "is a roof for my head. It is not a proper hat."

Neither of us was fluent enough in the other's language to make any fine distinctions of style. Since I had no hat with me except the clumsy pot-shaped pith helmet I was wearing, I offered him that, saying that I could manage with a "country hat," the kind that any of my carriers could fashion in a few minutes from palm thatch.

The chief shook his head at my offering.

"Your hat is a turtle-hat," he said. "It would make me feel that I crawl on the ground with my neck out in front of me. I do not like ground-crawl."

We looked at one another with the mute helplessness of those who want to communicate and can't manage it. Finally a helpful idea lighted his face, and he disappeared into his house. After a bit of banging of lids of wooden chests, he reappeared bearing aloft in his hands the remains of what had been at one time a high silk hat. Nothing remained of the crown except some rusted and broken wire supports. The hat band had fared better than the rest of the structure, but it was insect-chewed and green with mould. The crumpled brim was a sagging remnant of the original splendor. Even in its decrepity, the old top hat had a remnant of dignity.

"This now," said the chief, "is a *hat*. It is dead now, but it remains a hat. When I stand under this kind of hat, I am tree-tall. Put your eye on that big tree over there! When I wear this kind of hat, the top of me and the top of that tree stand even. We talk! You see now why I cannot satisfy with a hat like the one on your head. I am not wanting to feel myself low like a turtle."

I promised the chief that I would find him a top hat at the Liberian coast even if I had to snatch the President's own. I promised myself that I would try to cultivate in my own body the genuine experience of empathy which came so naturally to the chief. I stood before him in the African sun with my turtle-hat in my hand. As piercing as the rays of the tropical sun was the sudden revelation that during all of my experience in art I had never felt myself eye-level with a tall tree or belly-low with a turtle.

I had heard, as most art students must, that strong vertical lines suggest dignity and strength, that horizontals are restful and serene or suggest forward motion, and that diagonals are active and restless. I knew these things with my head and had even made some use of them in my designs, but I had never felt them as forces exerting themselves in my physical being. I had seen photographs of Gothic cathedrals and had been told that the soaring verticality expressed man's aspirations toward God. One can study a print and appreciate the *idea* of verticality with the mind, but one can't soar very high in bodily feeling within the limitations of even a page-high photograph.

I must have stood there in the sun for quite a while thinking about these things. The chief waited with admirable courtesy. He knew, in the wonderful way those people have of knowing, that I was not with him even though not two feet of distance separated us. I was inside of myself. He knew that when I was ready to return to him, I would. He continued to wait. When I became aware of his being there in front of me, I desperately wanted to tell him what I was thinking. I knew that because it was the natural thing for him to project his consciousness into trees or clouds or creatures, he would not be able to understand that this ability was foreign to me. Even with a fund of mutually understandable words, I did not think he would know what I was talking about.

Lacking anything significant to say to him, I merely said, "I thank you "

He touched my fingertips lightly with his own. The old eyes smiled and blinked like embers in his leathery face. I started slowly back to my hut with a distinct feeling that his intuition had penetrated to the core of what I could not explain and had thought him incapable of understanding.

I recall that I quickened my steps to the quick pace of his words as he called after me, "Walk you well, Ma! Walk you strong."

I knew at that moment how it feels to "walk strong." I suppose that in previous times I had walked this way in order to get where I wanted to go in a hurry, perhaps enjoying the brisk pace as a mild exhilaration. But never before had I been conscious of the thought, "This is the feeling of walking briskly. This is good." I had enjoyed a first lesson in empathy. Perhaps with practice, I might, while standing on the ground, feel myself eye-level with the top of a tall tree. I might be able to feel in my body the lazy float of a cloud or the slow swirl of blue smoke above the evening cooking fires or the staccato strokes of pestles beating rice in the mortars.

That conversation about a top hat was, I think, a sort of turning point in my own creative life. I considered writing about it in other books I have written, but I shied away because in the telling it seems slight and can give no more than a hint of the intense experience it was. Then too, I have always been suspect of sentences that begin with, "I feel." I have noticed that these two words usually are followed by a pause and then some fuzzy, half-formulated impressions too weak to stand on a good solid base of "I think." Such were the disciplines of my youth that I believed that thoughts which couldn't stand the clear light of good reasons had better be kept to oneself. A "felt" seemed the last resort of muddied logic. The old chief gave me a logical "felt," and I believe that everything I have tried to design since has been better because of it.

Back in the United States, I talked with a friend who seems to have an unusual talent for joyous living. She was telling about watching the start of the Ensenada boat race from Newport Harbor. The California sun was shining. The bay twinkled. The shore was lined with people. Little boats stood by as the larger ones prepared to take off. Helicopters hovered over the pageant in the bay.

"I don't know which thrilled me more," she said, "whether it was the heavy machinery of the copters buoyed up in the air and darting around like humming birds or the graceful hulls of the boats buoyed up by the water. First I was in the copters, scooting or dawdling, then in the yachts with the water holding me up, then back in the copters."

This American woman whose job is bookkeeping has the same talent for empathy as the old African chief. She "goes out and into" whatever attracts her. She will never be bored because she would not know how to cage her imagination.

"But what does this have to do with art?" You may ask. "Doesn't empathy have more to do with a philosophy of living than with creating a design or with furnishing a home?"

Perhaps the two can never be separate. When one throws a pot on the wheel, or weaves a cloth, or does a stitchery, or landscapes one's yard, whatever one is at the moment of doing enters into the thing that is done and is a part of it.

Among my own students those who make the most rapid design progress are those willing to try to feel in their muscles and nerves as well as in their emotions the equilibrium of horizontal rest, the push toward a vertical when arising from a chair, the dynamics of the diagonal when reaching, the axis of balance when standing with a book on the head. From this, the next step is to feel these stresses and strains and reposes in line and form.

THE ELEMENT OF LINE

As a practice in empathy, suppose we consider the basic design element of *line*. Each of us deals with line in some way every day. We cannot write a note to a friend, set a table, place a handkerchief in a pocket, spread a rug on the floor, arrange flowers in a bowl, or even seat ourselves in a chair without arranging and rearranging line. Becoming aware of the quality of lines all about us is the first step in learning to use line effectively. Drawing is only one example of the expressive potential of line.

Try sitting alone very quietly in your own living room. Let your glance rove, and start taking inventory of the existing lines. There are the inevitable structural lines. Stare for a while at nothing but a ceiling corner, and absorb into your senses the impact of this meeting at right angles of hard, straight lines. Feel the drama of these lines being forcibly stopped at their exact point of meeting.

If you can *feel* the thrust and then the "brake" of movement set up in the lines of any ordinary room, you have begun to be sensitive to line. You will never again think of a ceiling corner as nothing but a potential gathering place for cobwebs. It will have become a small drama.

The disappointing thing about a ceiling corner is that after all the activity and tension set up by the thrust and brake of line movement, nothing happens. It is like a drum-roll before a curtain-rise, but the curtain stays down. We are stimulated and excited, then let down. This is so deeply true that "to sit and stare at the ceiling" has become a description of despair.

It is precisely to avoid this build-up of line tension for no aesthetic purpose that contemporary architects have introduced the soffit or drop ceiling and the use of glass immediately under the ceiling so that the continuing beams can be seen carrying the line beyond the corner.

We may not be able to change the box-like ceiling corners of our rooms, but we can maneuver the tablecloth so that the lines are "with" the lines of the table, not in opposition. We can, perhaps, persuade the man of the family to fold his pocket handkerchief so the exposed linen square repeats the line of the pocket instead of making a bright, distracting triangle above the slot of the pocket opening. We can shift the diagonal rug so that its sides repeat and are harmonious with the direction of line set up by the walls. Having felt line-thrust as a force, we will use lines well.

Line language came long before the written word. We are astonished by the forceful, telling lines drawn on the walls of caves by prehistoric men who interpreted life and invoked magic with line drawings. Line is the easiest element of design to approach empathically—perhaps because man has used it for expressive purposes for thousands of years.

BALANCE

Balance, too, can be approached through empathy. Our bodies learned quite a lot about balance at the time we learned to walk. Walking becomes automatic long before one is adult, but it is possible to regain consciously the feel of balance by becoming aware of the walking process. Then one can project this awareness into what one designs or arranges.

David Vaughan, a talented artist living in California, tells how the feeling for balance developed in him while he was convalescent with a broken leg. For diversion a friend brought him some chunks of driftwood picked up at the beach. Having no work to occupy him, Mr. Vaughan began studying these water-sculpted forms with his hands as well as with his sight. He became curious about where the imaginary axis or center of gravity might be. They were too irregular to have a measurable center. By spinning them and studying the forms as they twirled and feeling himself into the motion as he watched, he "reached" the spot where the two differently formed halves seemed to center and balance. This, he says, set him off on a whole new approach to his work as a practicing artist.

When one achieves this kind of rapport with the principle of balance, one knows at once whether the fireplace at one end of a room is so heavy in scale that it seems to tip the opposite side of the room up at a slope. One knows at once whether the darks or the brights on one side of a composition balance those on the other. One is dragged lopsided by imbalance, but feels serene and at ease with the well-balanced. This is not measure by rule but physical response of the sort that lets us know without thought where our foot will meet the floor, how far we will lean forward when climbing a hill, how much we will brace ourselves against stiff blasts of wind, how to find our sea legs when afloat.

OTHER EMPATHIC RESPONSES

Sometimes the capacity for empathy is enlarged by reading those writers who have felt it most keenly. Thus I find evidences of the empathic response in many writers. Richard Jefferies, for example, knew how to put into words the ephemeral experience of losing one's separateness and becoming part of the whole universe. I hope you will take time to go to the library and search out Richard Jefferies. Walt Whitman also responded to the world empathically as is evident in the following lines:

> You vapors, I think I have risen with you,
> moved away to distant continents, and
> fallen down there for reasons,
> I think I have blown with you you winds;
> You waters I have finger'd every shore with you . . .[1]

In the beginning one may not be able to diffuse oneself widely enough to "finger every shore," but one can feel the force of a coiled fern frond springing into leaf or the push of a milkweed seed thrust from the pod. To be able to empathize with the common things about us brings that heightened awareness which is the beginning of all creative activity.

On February 20, 1962, millions of Americans squeezed into a small bell-shaped space capsule with astronaut John Glenn. They went through the burst of flame with him as he cast off from Cape Canaveral. They whirled in orbit. They made the fiery reentry into the earth's atmosphere. They dropped into the sea with him and were picked up by the destroyer Noa. Most of these persons had never heard or thought about empathy, but they were experiencing it in an intense way. They were *there,* and they were participating in everything that happened. The television set they watched or the radio they listened to were only the means of getting them there. They were not passive observers. They were participants.

A member of our Fellowship was empathizing with nature when he wrote the following stanza, which he later used as a basis of a line design.

[1] "Salut au Monde" in *Leaves of Grass,* New York, Heritage Press, copyright by Doubleday (no year given).

Clouds swirl and float.
I need no wings,
I WALK THE SKY!

In his painting he did not portray himself walking the sky. That would have ruined everything. What he did do was to invent lines which swirled with enough vigor to pull you into the painting.

The word *feeling* may be used to mean a sympathetic *emotional* state of responsiveness or an organic *physical* sensation, usually associated with the sense of touch. Empathy involves both types of feeling—the emotional and the physical. If you were emotionally involved in the heroic effort of our first man to go into orbit (and who was not?), you felt the cramped space of his quarters in your own body; you knew with your muscles and nerves as well as with your emotions.

5 Awareness through work

A flock of birds alights on a telephone wire. The unaware person will not give them a second tilt of his head. The alert person wants to know what kind of birds these are; he wants to accord them the pleasure of recognition. He notices how they have arranged themselves on the wire, the spaces between the birds, the pattern made by the group. They have become a momentary *event*. When awareness is at work, each day becomes a series of small delights which heighten life. A wonderful thing about awareness is that it multiplies of itself.

Indifference is a habit of mind leading to sloth and tedium. You can sentence yourself to be imprisoned by boredom, or you can liberate yourself to fervent interests. If indifference has become a personal habit, some deliberate and even strenuous conscious effort may be required. You will have to be your own self-starter. You can't drag along on the coat-tails of another's enthusiasm. You can't get any dividends out of something in which you never invest. Nothing is interesting unless you are interested in it. The interest has to come from you or it is nonexistent.

I recall the disbelief I felt when it was explained to me in school that if a great tree were to topple in the forest during a thunderstorm, there would be no sound unless an ear, human or animal, were there to convert the sound waves into the sensation of noise. There seemed something fraudulent about physics when it held that my ear or the ear of some other creature was auxiliary. I tried to reject the idea and was bothered by it for several adolescent years.

I can see now that many of the people I know do not subscribe to the idea that an interest resides in the mind of an individual and is not inherent in an object or activity. We say, "This is interesting," failing to think, perhaps failing to believe, that, "I am investing this with my interest." The *I* is the microphone which transforms and produces fervor and excitement and delight or which registers nothing at all. A change of scene, a journey, a new job, a new neighborhood, a new set of acquaintances may stimulate the *I*, but it is the *I* which gives or withholds, which transforms and amplifies or goes dead. A scene is not dreary unless we feel it dreary, and it is not beautiful unless we feel it beautiful. When I first saw the western deserts, I thought of them as depressing wastelands to be hurried through. Now I camp in them at every opportunity. The deserts have not changed much but I have.

What I saw when I disliked the desert was a panoramic view of rocks and sand and stunted bushes. What I have now is an experience of fossils and minerals and a sense of geology which has come alive through intimate association with the results of geologic time. I want to memorize the feel in my hand of a water-washed and polished pebble while I think about the waterway which coursed through this sand where I sit eons ago, and polished this pebble which I hold, this natural "sculpture for the hand" with its patina of desert varnish from its sun-baked years. As I hold this pebble (it is on my desk now), I feel an alliance with natural creation, and I am quietly and deeply happy.

Let us ask questions of rocks and make inquiry of the weeds and grasses. The stars are good company.

You ask, "What does this have to do with art? How can holding a rock in my hand help me draw a design or furnish my house with taste?"

My answer is that all art is a matter of the human spirit. It is not following a frayed set of rules, and it is not a blind obedience to pro-

Fig. 3. *Leaves and Bark*, bleach print, Rosita Montgomery. Photo by Lee Payne.

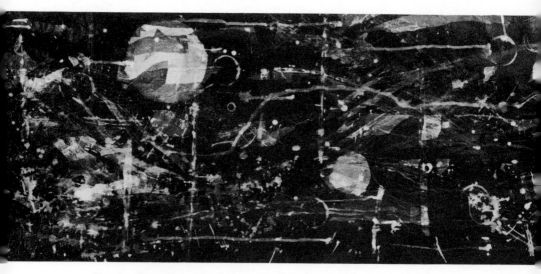

Fig. 4. *Outer Space*, freely done bleach print, Claudine Crittenden. Photo by Lee Payne.

fessionals who are quite certain of the excellence of their own taste. One has only to read that lively book by Russell Lynes, *The Tastemakers,*[1] to see that ideas about what is good taste are considerably less enduring than my rock from the desert.

What does seem to have endured in man throughout the centuries is not a shifting set of man-made rules for good design, but a reverence for the fundamental *laws of the universe.* Great artists of all times have felt the rhythms and forces and forms and proportions of nature and have expressed these, each in his own unique way.

Henry David Thoreau, the great American naturalist, said that he went to the woods because he wished to live deliberately.[2] Not many of us could manage to live alone in the woods for two years and two months beside a Walden pond as Thoreau did. In fact if this opportunity were offered, most of us would be appalled at the prospect. We would concentrate quickly on excuses for rejecting the proposal. Fortunately one does not have to become a recluse in order to become intimately familiar with natural form. We can absorb nature intensely in our own back yards. The growth patterns to be found in one weedy vacant lot are abundant. Familiarity often blinds us to the marvels of the commonplace. The intricate traceries of veins, the delicate pattern of their branching, the rhythm of progressively smaller repetitions of space intervals, the gradual thinning of line—all of these can be seen in a single fallen leaf. Anyone can acquire a sense of beautiful form and heighten his sensibility by making himself intimately familiar with natural objects.

AWARENESS OF NATURAL FORMS

How much silent reverence are you willing to accord these minuscule marvels of natural form? You will see them better and recall them longer if you memorize the smell and the feel in the hand as well as the visual aspects. The form of any particular leaf can be thoroughly memorized by the senses if you make a print or a rubbing and finally an arrangement of the recorded form. There are several methods of making prints. All of them are so simple that small children can carry them

[1] Russell Lynes, *The Tastemakers,* New York, Harper, 1949.
[2] *Walden and Other Writings of Henry David Thoreau,* New York, Random House (The Modern Library), 1950.

Fig. 5. *Our Friends*, planned bleach print, Virginia Horn. Photo by Lee Payne.

through during one pleasurable flurry of activity. The unexamined and the unexplored does not exist for us until we give it to ourselves. Prints and rubbings of natural objects are one way to do this.

Perhaps the simplest method of recording form is one which uses household bleach and dark tissue paper. The object to be printed is dipped into a weak solution of bleach. After the excess liquid is shaken or blotted from the object, it is dropped on dark paper. The bleaching action of the adhering liquid removes the pigment from the dark paper beneath the object. As one works with the bleach solution some of it is likely to drip onto the dark paper, forming interesting dots and blobs which tempt one to play freely with the method. One can spatter the paper by flipping the fingers or by dipping a brush in the solution and dragging it across the paper. The natural object with which we started has in this way led to free play and experiment with the material.

In Fig. 4 *Outer Space,* we see a mood statement which was achieved by beginning with accidental finger flippings and then developing an area with the same kind of activity, repeating the wrist and finger movements which resulted in the initial pattern.

34

F<small>IG</small>. 6. *Fish Print,* India ink rubbing, Rosita Montgomery. Photo by Lee Payne.

Invented forms cut from cardboard may be dipped in the bleach water and dropped in some planned arrangement on the dark paper. Fig. 5, *Our Friends,* was achieved in this manner.

In this simple kind of art fun we become aware of natural form; we become aware that rhythmic body movements can create a pleasing rhythmic pattern; we become aware that simple forms cut from cardboard can make amusing patterns.

Making fish prints has been an art in the Orient for many years. When making such prints, it is helpful to spray the admired fish with fixative before applying a surface coat of India ink with a brush. Rice paper is pressed against the ink-damp surface of the fish and then carefully lifted. After a little experimentation to get the best thickness of ink and a feel for the correct pressure of the hands on the paper, you will be able to record in minute detail the marvelous and intricate texturing of scales and fins.

You will enjoy experimenting with direct printing of numerous objects. Tempera paint may be applied directly to whatever one wishes to print, and then the object may be dabbed against paper. One begins to

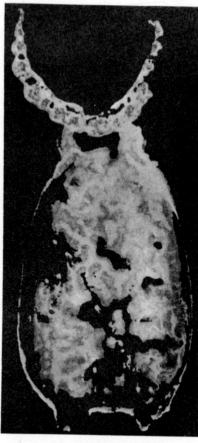

Fig. 7 (*left*). *Artichoke Warrior*, direct print, tempera, Virginia Harder. Photo by Lee Payne.

Fig. 8 (*right*). *Cactus Bush*, combined natural shapes, Rosita Montgomery. Photo by Lee Payne.

see not only the structure of growth forms but also unexpected re-semblances which pop up to amuse and excite. Virginia Harder found a Japanese warrior complete with helmet and scowl in an artichoke she halved and printed (Fig. 7).

The end of a cut stalk of celery and a halved cactus fruit, as com-bined by Rosita Montgomery, suggest fish when they are viewed in one position and contemplative bulls when seen as a vertical (Fig. 8).

Through using playful combinations one begins to see that shapes are expressive forms with design possibilities. This is a great forward step in understanding art. The beauty of a shape does not depend upon what it "looks like"; a shape is pleasing or it is not pleasing because of the kind of shape it is. We will talk more about this when we discuss form. Just now, I want you to continue having fun exploring all the shapes you can.

You will have a good time combining shapes, playing the textured rings of an onion, for instance, against the plain surface of a split red pepper pod (Fig. 9).

There are many other ways to record natural form and the uniqueness of found objects. Rubbings are delightful. Most of us have whiled away some time in grade school by stroking a pencil lead across a penny placed under a sheet of paper. Leaves, shells, feathers, bark, sliced fruit, vegetables, seed pods—all of these can be recorded in the same way. Wax crayons, in a choice of colors, may be used for your rubbings, which may be done either on paper or on fabric.

Fig. 9. *Plain and Ringed,* onion and pepper, direct print, Virginia Harder. Photo by Lee Payne.

37

Fig. 10 (*left*). *Leaf Rubbing*, crayon, Donna Read. Photo by Lee Payne.
Fig. 11 (*right*). *Crayon Rubbing*, wall hanging, Rosita Montgomery. Photo by Lee Payne.

One's eyes and senses widen as one watches the complex of delicate leaf veins grow under the fingers into a permanent record.

Rosita Montgomery made her rubbing of papyrus fronds on golden raw silk, using a black crayon and a green one to provide accents here and there (Fig. 11). It was done to hang on a dark cork fireplace wall in her living room. The rubbing conveys the feeling of wind-swayed willowy stalks in the sun.

A rubber roller or brayer will increase the possibilities of both the direct printing and the rubbing techniques. A few small dabs of block

Fig. 12. *Brayer People*, accidental figures, Donna Read. Photo by Lee Payne.

printing ink are squeezed out of the tube on a sheet of glass or a piece of aluminum foil. The brayer is rubbed over this until the ink is evenly distributed. Even before the ink is evenly disposed around the roller, you may want to make a few trial runs to determine whether unusual patterns will just happen of themselves. You might use two brayers of different widths to roll colors across the paper or fabric before doing any printing—a technique which sometimes results in interesting break-ups of space. We are not learning any "rules" at this point; we are just giving ourselves an opportunity to see which space divisions are interesting and which ones are monotonous. The darker tones in Rosita Montgomery's space experiment (Fig. 13) are caused by overlapping swaths of the inked brayers.

In direct printing the brayer is run over the object to be printed. In indirect printing the form to be printed is set in place *under* the paper or fabric. The inked brayer rolled across the top surface gives the imprint of the object beneath. Sliding the form and rerolling the brayer makes "ghost" or shadow forms appear.

By this time you have collected a great number of objects of natural beauty. You have concentrated on their various and infinitely varied forms. You have thought about which ones seem to enhance one another by being placed together. You have had a chuckle or two, I hope, at the surprising things which have emerged from the brayer or from combining natural forms in unique ways. You have begun to see form for its own sake. You have pushed forward. *You have begun by becoming aware.*

We have five senses and use them only partly, oh so partly. Dylan Thomas wrote a poem called "When All My Five and Country Senses See." We are learning "country sense" when we alertly investigate natural form.

One of the biggest satisfactions I have in teaching usually happens on a Monday morning. An *entire* family comes into the studio clutching a bundle of rubbings made after a Sunday together on the beach. An art activity has *made* their holiday. This truly is relating art to daily living.

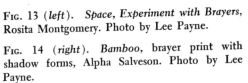

FIG. 13 (*left*). *Space, Experiment with Brayers*, Rosita Montgomery. Photo by Lee Payne.

FIG. 14 (*right*). *Bamboo*, brayer print with shadow forms, Alpha Salveson. Photo by Lee Payne.

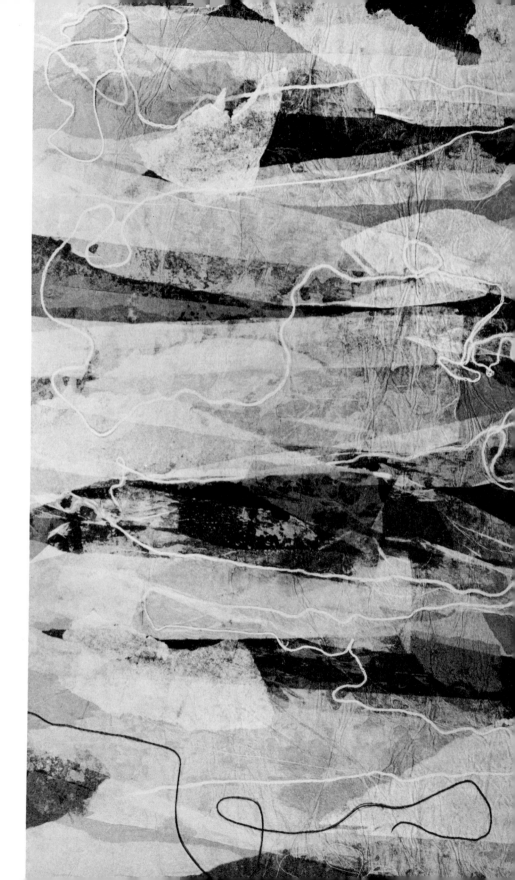

II *The arts of making*

6 Subjective approaches to design

It has seemed to us as we have explored and investigated and experimented with how to go about saying something with art materials that all of the design approaches we know about can be reduced to two basic approaches which sometimes overlap.

For lack of a more descriptive word, the first might be called *subjective*. It may start with a mood or an idea, but the image, either abstract or figurative, evolves from the subconscious. It is not calculated. It is not done knowingly "with the top of the mind." It grows under the fingers. Often the materials in purely accidental happenings determine the next step, and the next. One responds to material happenings sensuously, allowing one event to grow into another until the series of events, responded to by all the senses, have produced something which

45

GOSHEN COLLEGE LIBRARY
GOSHEN, INDIANA

the conscious part of the mind seizes upon in great excitement and begins to direct.

This is a difficult process to explain to one who has never had the *experience;* there is no way to tell *about* it and be understood, just as there is no way for a saint to describe a state of religious ecstasy to those of us who are not saints. I should not have the temerity to approach the subjective method were it not for its proven effectiveness in our own group. Ardent, imaginative beginners, as well as accomplished artists, have had success with subjective approaches. It is a popular way of working these days.

Perhaps I can give you some idea of the way the subjective approach has worked for me in the use of words. I was sitting at the table with guests one night in 1957. I'm afraid I was daydreaming to soft background music and candle light when I should have been listening to the conversation. From out of the murmur at my right I heard only one word. That word was *butter.* Did some one wish me to pass the butter? I came to with a start. That one word heard out of context hit with thunderclap force. Guiltily, I located the butter. Everyone about the board was chatting.

"Do you really think the cholesterol in butter is harmful?" I tried to relax into relieved hostessdom. My lapse of attention had gone without notice. The word *butter* kept ringing in my ears with annoying persistence. After the guests departed, I began wondering how butter had figured in the stories of the Old Testament. If I found out, the word might stop plaguing me. I came upon this:

> . . . *when my children were about me:*
> *When I washed my steps with butter,*
> *and the rock poured me out rivers of oil,*
> *Then I said I shall die in my nest,*
> *And I shall multiply my days as the sand.*[1]

This was poetry. I memorized it. Then I went to bed. But not to sleep. Words kept fastening themselves in chain-link fashion to other words, something like this: *rivers of oil* . . . what kind of oil? Palm oil of Africa, red as jasper, shining in the sun when it is poured from a gourd. *My children were about me* . . .

[1] Mary Ellen Chase, *The Bible and the Common Reader,* New York, The Macmillan Company, 1944, p. 217.

For several months previous to this I had been toying with the idea of writing a story about a woman in the hinterland of Africa, a nurse who defied her superiors and the customs of the tribal people by saving the lives of twin babies who are usually left out in the bush to die. She loved the sweet Danish butter which came to the coast in flat little tins which were so expensive that one couldn't afford them very often. Usually she and the children made do with palm oil. She died as she wished, in her bush home with the children about her, but her days were multiplied in the influences she made real during many devoted years.

Well, there it was! My story had been building up in me for a long time but in a vague way. I had not all of the story, of course; novels don't come that easy. But enough, something to start on. It turned out to be the end of the book, not the beginning. Children, butter, oil, die in my nest. . . .

I jumped out of bed and sat down at the typewriter. Before morning I had the entire last chapter of *The Silk Cotton Tree,* the only chapter in the finished book which is fairly satisfactory to me now. The other chapters had to be calculated to join on to what was done in one excited spurt. The magic never settled down on me during the remainder of the book.

Now I am quite sure that this is not the approved way to write a novel. It should be outlined, the texts say, planned, and the plan developed. This is the exact opposite of what happened in me because I heard *butter* and could not sleep until one word had yeasted into many.

I am strongly in favor of "yeasting" because every week I see how thoroughly the members of our Fellowship have astonished themselves by using a subjective approach. Some of us do better with the opposite approach, the objective. I believe all of us should give good trial to both so as to discover which is better suited to our own temperament.

If one is going to try a subjective approach, how does one start? It seems to me that materials are the clue and the beginning. In writing, words are the material. In designing, papers, paints, whatever one chooses to work with, are the materials. One brings to the materials, as one brings to anything, all the layers of thought and feeling which have made up the store of life experience. These are dormant but ready to spring into activity and influence the material as it is manipulated.

In this chapter we will be looking at various spontaneous or subjective approaches to design. The first approaches we discuss are limited to

47

particular mediums—collage and encaustic; the other approaches are of wider applicability.

COLLAGE

I know of few artists who are able to "see" a design in its entirety before it is started. The creative person makes a beginning, keeps himself intently alert and aware as the work progresses, and often allows the material and the emerging forms to lead him to quite a different statement than was intended in the beginning.

Collage, the art of pasted paper or fabric, is a medium in which the material can lead you all along the way. Your collages are more likely to be successful if they are started without preplanning. Let each move quickly and impulsively to its own conclusion and fulfillment. Think about what you have done after it seems finished rather than before you start. Additions can always be made if you don't like what you've done.

When making collages, thin tissue papers in brilliant colors give handsome results. The overlapping of the semitransparent tissues automatically relates the colors, one to another. If the color used on the top surface seems to make a spot too dark or too bright it can be lifted off before the adhesive dries, leaving only a faint dye-stain. In addition to the colored tissues you will need a brush, a bottle of concentrated starch for adhesive, and a background paper. Shelf paper will do.

Among our group, Mrs. Alpha Salveson has produced collages which have earned her the honor of one-man shows in Florence and Rome. Here is her own description of how she goes about making a collage:

I have better luck when I work in an intense, almost frenzied haste, enjoying the excitement of seeing the third color emerge when two different colors of tissue are overlapped. The only planning I do is to arrange the tissue in order of the tones, usually from dark to light. If I am going to work in reds, oranges, yellows, the warm tones, I might have brown for my deepest tone. If I feel like working in cool colors, blue-greens and blues, say, I might use dark gray or even black for my deepest tone.

Once the paper is arranged in tonal order in front of me, I start to tear it, trying to move my fingers nimbly to get interest and excitement from the changes of direction of the tearing. The only rule I follow, if it can be called a rule, is to get three long strips of the darkest tone going entirely across my background paper, although not necessarily parallel to one another.

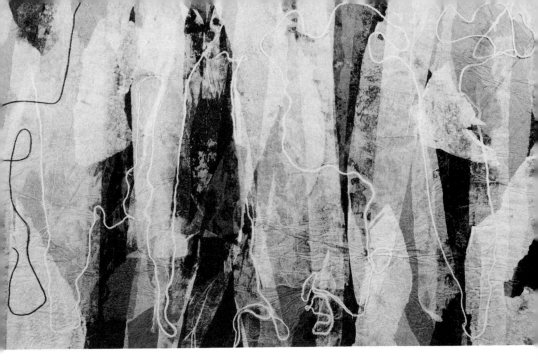

Fig. 15. *Collage*, Alpha Salveson. Photo by Lee Payne.

Fig. 16. *Collage*, Alpha Salveson. Photo by Lee Payne.

These are adhered by quick strokes of the brush which has been dipped in starch. The starch can be swiped over the top of the paper without disturbing its position.

Torn shapes are more likely to be interesting than cut shapes. Scissors tend to get between me and the medium. The more facile the fingers the better the chance of good shapes. There is an immediate pleasure just in tearing the crisp paper.

After the three beginning strips of the dark tone are torn and stuck down, I begin tearing and pasting the next tone, letting the forms overlap as they will. As I build toward the surface, tone after tone, I sometimes dip string or yarn in the starch and let it fall on the paper with a rhythmic motion of the hand. Sometimes I use bits of rice paper or scraps from the rubbings which I love to make of natural forms.

My torn strips of paper protrude over the edges of my background paper, but I do not trim them until I have set my collage behind a matte and stood off from it to see whether any areas have been neglected and whether the darks seem to balance out. If I am happy with what I have done, I let the starch dry, and then I press the back of the collage with an iron. Sometimes the length of my clothesline is hung with collages put out to dry.

In speaking of Mrs. Salveson's collages, Dr. Knud Voss, distinguished art critic of Copenhagen, says:

In this pictorial art three factors assert themselves above all; color, composition, and the space created in the picture. The last-named is not the least important. It is space with deep-lying lines and wide planes. Opposed to this spaciousness, yet together with it, the most delicate lyrical moods live, called to life especially by the colors. She entrusts everything to the one who will concentrate his attention on her pictures. Faced with them you seem to be to an odd degree happily in the power of your imagination. Immense visions, landscapes, figures, heaven and earth come into existence by the consideration.[2]

Beautiful colors, exciting shapes, and interesting spacing—these are what Mrs. Salveson aims to achieve in her work. She does not try to make the shapes she tears resemble any natural object. Sometimes recognizable forms do appear quite by accident, and these may be developed toward further recognizability. When shapes appear by surprise, they occur in a way one would never think of drawing which presents more of a challenge to the imagination. When the torn shapes do not suggest concrete images, the collages are perhaps even more likely to evoke "immense visions . . . heaven and earth."

[2] Knud, Dr. Voss, *Brochure, Numero,* Florence, Italy, 1961.

Some collage artists like to stretch burlap over the kind of stretcher used by oil painters. After the burlap is stapled in place, the paper is applied to it, permitting the burlap texture to become part of the artistic statement. A thin coat of plastic may be sprayed on the surface to give a protective finish.

Recently Mrs. Salveson has been experimenting with the use of organdy instead of colored tissue, working in the same manner which has brought her renown with paper collage except that she cuts the organdy, since it will not tear freely into irregular fragments. Using organdy, which is partly transparent, she can achieve the same pleasant quality of overlapped forms. White organdy can be colored in related tones by running an inked brayer or roller over the surface of the fabric.

ENCAUSTIC

The extensive investigations which the Fellowship made into encaustic painting were triggered by a grade-school project. Paula Mont-

FIG. 17. *Collage*, Alpha Salveson. Photo by Lee Payne.

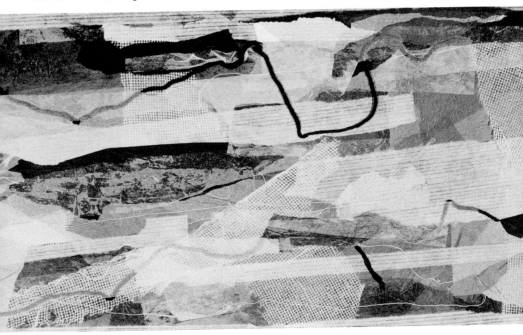

gomery, aged eleven, brought home a colorful paper panel which excited the entire group when her mother presented it to us. Paula had shaved the stubs of wax crayons onto a sheet of waxed paper, covered this with another layer of waxed paper, then pressed it lightly with a cool iron. The crayon shavings, partly melted, which were the filling in this waxed paper sandwich, glowed through the paper like a scattering of jewels. Here was obviously something which we should look into and carry farther.

With this as a beginning, we set about to research and experiment. We learned that the word "encaustic" (from a Greek word for "burnt-in") is used to describe paintings in which wax is the chief ingredient. We got into a lot of exciting history during our reading. We learned that Egyptian paintings were done with wax on stone at least five thousand years ago. We studied Egyptian mummy paintings. We found out that in olden days ships were decorated with encaustic paintings because of the resistance of wax to salt water. Many art historians believe that the use of encaustic explains the freshness of the wall paintings of Pompeii. The old formula for encaustic is thought to have been lost during the Middle Ages. Now we had a real challenge.

We discovered that we could get away from the rather dull appearance of the top layer of waxed paper. This was our first advance. We started exactly as Paula had, then pulled the paper sandwich apart. By choosing whichever sheet of waxed paper had the more wax adhering to it, and laying that sheet face down on rice paper, then pressing lightly, we had a new top paper and a more beautiful one for the front surface of the picture. Some of these works had a lyrical quality which was the result of chance happenings, but what bothered all of us was that we could not build on these chance happenings. We set out to find methods of control.

Mrs. Kathryn Hossack discovered that after the wax papers were separated, she could do some direct manipulation of whatever had happened previously, by drawing directly on the surface with the tip of a crayon. These additions were not too much disturbed by the final pressing once she had found out the correct iron temperature and the exact amount of pressure to exert. Her *Cliff by the Sea* is a tone poem in greys and grey-greens. This is an example of letting accidental happenings develop into consciously controlled statements. She lives by the sea; the sound and smell of the sea is an everyday experience. She did

Fig. 18. *Autumn Leaves*, organdy collage stitchery, Alpha Salveson. Photo by Lee Payne.

Fig. 19. *Crayon Panel*, encaustic, Paula Montgomery. Photo by Lee Payne.

not set out to do rocks and waves but when the accidental smoothings of the iron across the wax paper suggested them, the life experience of water and rock and clinging growth on the rock was there ready to take over.

Mrs. Brenda Wilkinson, well-known enamellist and also a member of the Fellowship, plunged into further research. Here is her own description of what she did (after extensive reading), and how she directed her investigations:

I wanted *control* of the colors and the placements. I started my experiments on pieces of wood placed in the kitchen oven. I didn't begin to get what I wanted until I thought of cutting the crayons into pieces instead of shaving them. I found that hard wood is a better background than soft wood. I also discovered that great care must be taken lest the wax run off the board and ignite the oven. (A "tray" formed out of foil is a good precaution.) A temperature of about 250 degrees gives the wood a good chance to absorb the wax as it melts. I could reach into the oven and stir the wax all about or leave it alone. When it is first removed from the oven, the wax is liquid enough to blend and swirl simply by moving the board in a slow rhythmic motion.

When the wax has cooled it has an all-over rather dull look. If I had not scratched into the surface, I might have abandoned this method. One scratch with an old dentist tool showed me that all the brilliance of the crayons was hidden beneath the surface film. This scratching or graffito technique has unlimited possibilities.

My next experiment was with a soldering iron. I cut the crayons lengthwise, placed them where I wished on the board, and melted the colors one by one. I could melt them less and have thick lines or melt them more and let the color spread. I could drag the wax when I pleased.

The finished work can be given a "warm over" with just enough heat to soften the contours and add to the unity without loss of the placement and brilliance of the color. I found that polishing the finished surface with a soft cloth brought out an increased brilliancy of color.

In Brenda Wilkinson's *Dune Birds* (Fig. 21) the grain of the wood beneath the wax is vaguely discernible, one of the chance happenings that contributed to the total effect. The colors have a special brilliance because light penetrates *into* the wax, as it cannot do into opaque paint. The mount for this composition is an orange burlap keyed to the earth yellows and reds of the dunes and the birds.

Others of the group found it possible to apply the wax directly with a

FIG. 20. *Cliff by the Sea*, encaustic, Kathryn Hossack. Photo by Lee Payne.

Fig. 21. *Dune Birds*, encaustic on wood, Brenda Wilkinson. Photo by Lee Payne.

Fig. 22. *Swedish Spring Flowers*, graffito encaustic, Karin Berg. Photo by Lee Payne.

brush. After carefully melting the crayons, they kept them liquid by placing the container over the candle in a coffee warmer.

Mrs. Karin Berg has been especially successful in combining the scratched into (graffito) effects with impasto, which is the thick use of the medium. In Fig. 22, her *Swedish Spring Flowers*, we have both thick masses of wax raised above the surface of the board and scratched lines going deep into the surface, almost down to the board itself. While respecting the painted surface, she has achieved tremendous textural effects in her statement.

I hope I have been able to convey some of the excitement and adventure we have had with this investigation. We found that the encaustic technique could produce color both brilliant and soft at the same time, and that it allowed for conscious manipulation, which we had not thought at first. We are sure that there is still more to be learned about painting with wax. We know we have not even scratched the surface of what could be done with the medium. We will come back to it some day and carry it further. Meanwhile there are a thousand or so other investigations we must make. A dozen lifetimes would not be enough to carry out the ideas we already have, and every week a whole new crop of ideas springs into being. We have read in the newspapers that some people in the world suffer from boredom. We simply could not believe this were it not that some of the Fellowship can vaguely recall that their own lives were not always as alive as now.

SUBJECTIVE USE OF A COMPASS

A compass may seem a cold and precise instrument to use in any but a calculated way. However the Fellowship has discovered that compass doodles are good imagination-stretchers.

We began by twirling the compass until we felt at home with it as an instrument. We enjoyed learning how to divide a circle into three, four, five, six or any practical number of parts, using only the compass. We began to understand why the ancient Greeks found entertainment in seeing what they could do with only a compass and ruler. The enjoyment we had from this part of our work came mostly from learning to use the tool in an expert way. In the beginning many students pick up the compass as though it were a dead mouse. We think of ourselves as a nation of tool users, but few women are. There is a sensuous pleasure

FIG. 23 (*left*). *Compass Pixie*, Paula Montgomery. Photo by Lee Payne.

FIG. 24 (*right*). *Compass Doodle and Emergent Form*, Marilyn Solomon. Photo by Lee Payne.

FIG. 25. *Repeating and Overlapping Forms*, Marilyn Solomon. Photo by Lee Payne.

in twirling until the compass seems a proper tool, which is to say until it seems like an extension of one's own fingers.

Our next step was to look at each segment of the divided circle as a separate form. We placed tracing paper over our work and traced one segment, any segment. Then we studied what had been traced. What did it suggest? A leaf, a fish, the body of a bird, the head of a creature? Perhaps this one segment did not suggest anything at this stage. We shifted the tracing paper and traced another segment, possibly joining it to the first segment, perhaps overlapping the forms, perhaps tracing it at a distance from the first attempt.

When using this technique if your imagination doesn't visualize something, it is quite likely that the lively imagery of a child will. This method is great art fun for the entire family. In Fig. 23 we see the pixie Paula Montgomery found in her mother's compass twirls.

Marilyn Solomon had traced only one segment of her compass doodle when she saw that with a few additions here and there she had the body of a bull (Fig. 24). Perhaps if we had not been studying the prehistoric paintings of the Lascaux caves shortly before this, she would not have seen the bull torso. Now we had a bull, a very fine bull, but what should we do with him? One good solution was to vary the size and overlap the forms (Fig. 25). The next and final step was to decide what medium to use to get the composition in permanent form. Mrs. Solo-

Fig. 26. *Compass Bulls*, mosaic, Marilyn Solomon. Photo by Lee Payne.

59

Fɪɢ. 27. *Compass Foliage*, Esther Dendel. Photo by Arlie Toulouse.

mon decided upon mosaic (Fig. 26). Notice that she used some partial forms, "ghosts," both light and dark, to activate otherwise empty spaces of the picture.

We could fill pages just listing the provocative forms we have found in our compass twirlings, but we want you to have the fun of finding what's there yourself.

It is possible to cover the picture area by partially repeating motifs as I have done in Fig. 27 with compass shapes which happened to suggest foliage.

Sometimes unusual forms evolve from the compass without the use of tracing paper. When Sylvia Mello started to twirl, it was without thought of an angel or any other definite form. What simply happened suggested an angel to her active imagination (Fig. 28). The straight lines were added with a ruler to repeat the straight lines of the frame. The composition is being done in mosaic for a headboard over her small grandson's bed.

The members of our Fellowship who work with Scouts and with 4-H Clubs have brought in stacks of designs done by children who have placed tracing paper over their compass twirlings and evolved imaginative forms from them. This is art play not only for families but for whole groups of people. There is play spirit in it, and this we need in our world, now more than ever.

Fig. 28. *Impudent Angel*, mosaic design, Sylvia Mello. Photo by Arlie Toulouse.

PLAY WITH NEGATIVE SHAPES

Suppose that what you have in mind is to make a stitchery using, say, bottle forms. You are going to cut many bottles out of folded paper. You snip and snip. This one seems too fat for its height. The next one seems too thin. Another seems too elaborate, and you think you will try simplifying the form. In working this way (objectively), you are making, as a by-product, all sorts of scraps, big and little, to which you pay no attention.

Next you arrange the bottle shapes on a background, overlapping them at varying distances. You raise some of them and lower some of them in order to get a good "skyline" and an interesting base-line. You are working in reference to the boundaries of the background. When you have finished the arrangement, the bottle shapes are the *positive* shapes of the design. The areas around them we might call the *negative* shapes; negative is a poor word, however, because what happens in these negative spaces is just as important as what is going on with the positive design shapes.

While Tanya Baker was cutting mountains of paper to get shapes she wanted, an outside door opened, and a gust of wind fluttered and swirled the cut paper, bottle shapes, and scraps from the cutting all over the room. She gathered them up and started sorting. While she was doing this, she noticed that she had some splendid shapes in the scraps. In great excitement she started to arrange them. What she had when she had finished was a rooster who seems to have some of the wind from the opened door fluttering his tail (Fig. 29). The scraps made a scrappy cock which she would never have thought of doing except for the accident of the wind.

The Fellowship applauded Tanya's efforts by making a project out of her method. All of us cut bottle shapes and then threw the bottles away! (We could have used any shape with ins and outs.) From the scraps that fell away from the bottles, we made whatever our imagination suggested. We had elephants, giraffes, cows, trolls, clowns, and processions. What all of them had in common was a gay, spontaneous, lively quality. This came, I think, from the spirit of play which is the spirit behind this approach.

I wish we had room for a thousand photographs so that you could see all that happened using this approach. Tanya Baker and Merion Seeley used colored construction paper in five colors instead of the usual newspaper for the experiment which resulted in their *Little King Totem* (Fig. 30). The planned cut-outs were all discarded, and the Little King was assembled from the bits of paper which fell on the rug while they worked. Only the ruler lines were added deliberately. *Little King Totem* is now being made into a mosaic for the Orange County hospital, after winning a design competition for "a panel which will give the patients a happy feeling." We think the happiness that went into the doing of it shows in what was done and that this often happens when one works with joy and a delight in discovery.

THE SCRIBBLE

If you will collect the scribbles you make on a pad beside the telephone while you are talking into it, you will notice that each scribble will reflect something of the quality of the conversation. It may be nervous and staccato or relaxed and flowing. The unplanned scribble or doodle is an intimate statement with great design possibilities.

FIG. 29 (*left*). *Scrap Rooster*, stitchery, Tanya Baker. Photo by Lee Payne.

FIG. 30 (*right*). *Little King Totem*, Merion Seeley and Tanya Baker. Photo by Lee Payne.

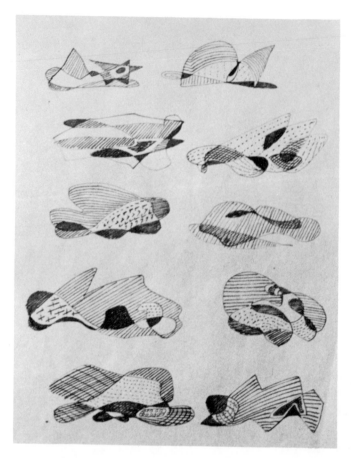

Fig. 31.   *Shaded and Textured Scribbles*, David Vaughan. Photo by Arlie Toulouse.

Fig. 32.   *Scribble*, Tanya Baker. Photo by Lee Payne.

One needs to make many scribbles and then shade and texture them in various ways. As often a scribble which seems to have "nothing in it" will come to life if one shades the forms within the overall shape.

The best doodles seem to happen when the paper is large enough to permit the drawing to be done with the entire arm, the goal being to make large free swings in continuous movement, returning the end of the line at last toward the source. Stand your scribbles around the house for a few days so that you can return to them in differing moods at different times of the day. Turn them sideways or upside down. Ask the children of the neighborhood what they can find in them.

Fig. 33.   *Scribble Stitchery*, Tanya Baker. Photo by Lee Payne.

To protect a promising scribble from getting lost during changes, it is wise to work on a tracing paper placed over the original drawing.

You may lift certain shapes out of a scribble as Tanya Baker did in her whimsical stitchery (Fig. 33), or you may take out certain sections, maintaining the same relationships which the forms happened to assume in the original.

One of the best things about the scribble approach is that it is play activity, relaxed, not solemn. In it there is no grim assertion that "I've got to get a design out of this." In the just-for-fun and what-is-it mood we often arrive at our most original statements.

65

LEADINGS FROM THE TOOL

"An unfamiliar tool, an inadequate musical instrument, but also a physically uncontrollable hand may contradict imagination, and, in the earliest moments of a dawning idea, may ruthlessly put it out."

Susanne Langer, in *Feeling and Form*[3]

"One works in holiness, and he raises up the sparks which hide themselves in all tools."[4]

Martin Buber

In my father's workshop were many tools. Before I was as tall as a large handsaw is long, these tools exerted a tremendous hypnotic effect upon me. I could not resist them, even though the workshop was forbidden terrain unless my father was there. There was a great wooden chest where each handsaw and plane and square had a special niche of its own. There was a rack where each chisel and plier had its leather loop to hold it in place. Nothing was ever tumbled about or helter-skelter. This was not the fancy kind of workshop men have now, with peg board and power tools and cupboards with sliding doors. It was a dilapidated old shed, hidden from the house by the more imposing corn-crib. Yet I have never felt more awe and reverence in a church than I felt in that old shed.

I saw the shredded sawdust fall from beneath the saw as my father worked; I saw the accurate pencil line on wood "eaten" by the steady progress of the blade; I saw the thin curls that fell from a plane; I smelled the delicious odor of worked wood. More important, I saw that the father who did this work was not the same man as the father who milked cows or hitched up a team of horses to go to the field. There was an astonishing transformation in him, a kind of radiating joy, as soon as he approached his tools. The truth is that my father was born to be a fine craftsman. He was not meant to till the fields; that was labor to him. Making things, fixing things, was joyous work.

I wanted to separate wood with a saw myself. When the opportunity occurred, I would approach the shed by a devious path, take the smallest of the saws from the chest, draw a line on a board, and attempt to

[3] Susanne K. Langer, *Feeling and Form*, New York, Scribners, 1953.
[4] *Man and God*, Victor Gollancz, ed., Boston, Houghton Mifflin, 1951.

follow it with accuracy. Every time I did this my act became known, even though I carefully replaced the saw and swept up every crumb of sawdust. From this I deduced that the tools communicated with my father in some secret language known only to them, that they "reported on me." My awe and respect increased.

One night I dreamed that the biggest saw approached my bed and began of itself to saw me in two without any arm to guide it. In those days, parents did not take children disturbed by fantasies to a psychiatrist; they just tried to figure out the common-sense remedy. I was given a saw of manageable size, the saw was given a special place "to live" near the other saws, and I was permitted to go openly to the shed to use it, provided nothing was left in disorder.

In Africa I learned from my craftsmen friends that tools are sacred. Because they accepted me as a fellow-craftsman, I was able to see sacrifices of rice and white chickens made to tools. I was living in a village one time when a man was found dead with the mark of a sledge in his skull. When I inquired privately—for one is careful how one speaks of death among these people—what had happened, I was told that the man, who was an apprentice to the blacksmith, had "spoiled" (profaned in some way) the tool. The tool had "retaliated" by "knocking" the man while he slept. Tools are thought to have the power to go about on their own, and a smithy is the most sacred spot in a village—so sacred that no one may apprehend a criminal while he takes refuge there.

I would like to know from those who study such matters whether my childish dream of an unguided saw wreaking vengeance on me while I slept did not have its origin in some ancient racial memory which is still accepted as factual in Africa.

In the *Munakata* volume of the Library of Japanese Art we read:

The elder Munakata was a craftsman in the old tradition, and he kindled his forge with a sense of ancient ritual. Hundreds of years before, it had been quite clear that the natural processes were controlled by the nature gods. A man who possessed the mysteries of a craft—whether building a house, brewing saké, or making a sword—was nothing less than a priest with power over those gods. When the primeval smith invoked the spirits of the forge, his Shinto rituals embodied the one right way to make a sword. Now we have dispensed with the gods and call it science, but for centuries, in Langdon Warner's words, the right way was the religious way.

The old forms die out, and Munakata's father was not called priest, but he felt toward his forge as priest to altar.[5]

We have lost our religious awe of tools, but we would add to life if we would regain a profound respect for them.

In using a tool we give evidence of our humanity. Of all the attributes which distinguish man from the beasts, one of the most important is that man is a tool-using animal. We think of ourselves as a nation of

Fig. 34. Mary Jean Stoddard at her loom. Iowa State University Photo Service.

[5] *Munakata,* Rutland, Vermont, Charles E. Tuttle.

great tool-users. The truth is that we are more a nation of gadget-pushers. The vacuum cleaner is not a tool in the deep sense of the word. It is an efficient gadget for cleaning a rug. When we pull the end of the extension cord from its moorings and repair the damage with a screwdriver, we have made a simple use of a tool. It is through the crafts that we recover tool-sense and the pleasure of manipulating them.

The first of all tools is the human body itself, with all its complexities of nerves and muscles and tendons. The skillfully handled tool becomes an extension of the body, whether that tool is a tile nipper, a jeweler's saw, a needle, a chisel, a pen, or a plane.

In the story of Mary Jean Stoddard's loom we have a beautiful example of the life-increasing potential of the craftsman's tool.

Mary Jean Stoddard got the idea for making her own loom while she was attending the Pi Beta Phi-University of Tennessee Craft Workshop. She saw looms that boys of high school age had made at the Settlement School, "If those boys can make looms I can, too," Mary Jean reasoned.

Back at Iowa State University for her senior year as a major in Applied Art, she checked over her plans with Miss Fisher, her weaving teacher. This is what she says about it:

Building the loom took over a hundred hours—at home nights, weekends, Christmas vacation. I worked like a Trojan. I planned the proportions considering my own height and reach. I combined different characteristics of looms I saw at Gatlinburg and made some innovations of my own. The back beam is far away from the harness so I can sit in there on a little stool that fits over the treadles. Dad got terribly interested in it. He understood it not through weaving but through applying simple physics. The total cost ran to about eighty dollars. It's solid black walnut. *I wanted a piece of furniture as well as a machine.* In a home of mine, the loom will be what the piano was to mother!

There was a time in this country when almost every man owned a jackknife. Men sat around stoves in country stores and whittled. In the summertime they would sit in the shade of a great tree, talking a little sometimes, but mostly just whittling. I have seen the lawn around the courthouse of a southern mountain town ankle-deep in shavings on a Saturday afternoon. I would like to see that again and in more places. I would like to start a crusade for the revival of whittling. I would like to have every boy and girl who is old enough to handle a jackknife own a good one.

Sometimes the only thing these mountain men whittled were shavings. But sometimes one of them would whittle *something*. This happens once in a while in other places, too. Arlie Toulouse picked up a waste scrap of wood from the boatyard where he works and in his hands it became an expressive graceful bird (Fig. 35).

Jo Dendel picked a length of discarded telephone pole out of the woodbox. Within the solid mass he saw the form of an old African chief's head, and he released this from the wood (Fig. 36), remembering his recent experiences with African people. He was led both by the material and by the tool.

As one works with different tools, one begins to see that the nature of the tool operating on the material exerts itself on the form of the final expression. Many home workshops have lathes. The lathe can lead one to an expression in wood that is quite different from a whittling. Every sort of amusing creature can emerge when whimsy operates with the symmetry of the lathe. We see this plainly in Fig. 37, a delightful rooster which "grew" in Professor Mabel Fisher's class at Iowa State University.

LINE OVER MASS

Artists have been concerned for many years with trying to get a sense of movement in their compositions. One device which helps is the use of a line which, instead of bounding a shape, moves freely in and out of the shape.

Line over mass can be used in either a preplanned or a subjective way. Our Fellowship has experienced the greatest excitement using it subjectively. We usually start with a collage done in the manner Mrs. Salveson has described (pp. 48, 50). We turn the collage in every direction to discover what subject matter, if any, is suggested. In almost every collage there are half-hidden, barely suggested forms. Finding them is a wonderful imagination-stretching exercise. What one discovers is usually related to what one has been thinking about just previously. During the Christmas season we tend to find magi and madonnas. During the summer we may find bathers, surfers, or seascapes in the same collages.

We place tracing tissue over the collage to experiment with establish-

FIG. 35. *Bird*, carving, Arlie Toulouse. Photo by Arlie Toulouse.

FIG. 36. *Aye, my people!* carving, Jo Dendel. Photo by Arlie Toulouse.

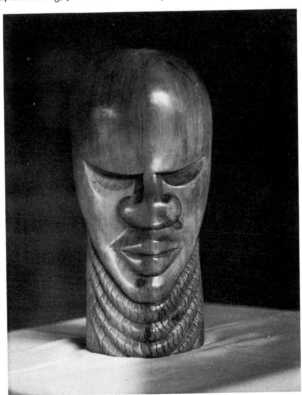

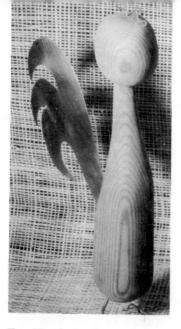

FIG. 37. *Lathe Rooster*, by a student in Professor Mabel Fisher's class at Iowa State University. Photo by Iowa State University Photo Service.

FIG. 38. *Wing and Wave*, collage and felt-pen, Gladys Howatt. Photo by Lee Payne.

ing the subject matter we wish to bring out. When we have what we want, we establish the line over the collage with a felt-nib marking pen. The areas of color in the collage provide the mass over which we draw the line. We try to vary the thickness of the lines: fat, thin, or tapered. The tapered line gives a front-back-forward again movement. We experiment on the tracing paper to see where the ink line may most effectively move into and out of the shapes.

In Fig. 38, *Wing and Wave,* Gladys Howatt built additional tissue paper onto the surface of her collage to further delineate the birds before she added the line. Both the wings and the waves "move" through this blue and green composition because of the activity of the lines.

HAIKU AND OTHER INTUITIVE APPROACHES TO DESIGN

In the previous pages we have discussed how the manipulation of materials and the leadings of tools can bring us into surprising art expressions. We have not said much about the state of mind in which such creation occurs. Designing intuitively might be described as a sort of "state of grace" to which all artists aspire, though more seems to have been written about it by philosophers and psychiatrists than by artists. Many artists who have the experience are not articulate enough to put it in words. We have the French philosopher Jacques Maritain writing about the "incommunicable world of creative subjectivity,"[6] and even though he calls this "incommunicable," he has a lot of wonderfully interesting things to say on the subject. I have read his book at least six times, and during every reading a little more comes through to me.

We have Dr. Sigmund Freud's discoveries about the "oceanic state," a feeling of being one with the universe, and the elaboration of this idea by many psychiatrists who have followed Freud.

And we have the insights of William Blake, a master in lyric poetry and in prose as well as with the engraving tool. There is a lively, renewed interest in Blake these days. I hear groups of students discussing his work and ideas over their coffee in the student lounge. I suspect this is because we feel especially, in these times, a need to recover the intui-

[6] Jacques Maritain, *Creative Intuition in Art and Poetry,* New York, Pantheon Books, 1953 (Bollingen Series xxxv.1).

tive quality of our lost childhood. We are as frightened in our time by the insensibility we see all about us as Blake was in his.

We pick up a volume of Blake hopefully. Perhaps it is *The Portable Blake,* or perhaps it is the beautiful larger volume of *Blake's Illustrations to the Divine Comedy.* We may find it difficult to pick our way through the maze of symbols which Blake invented as a sort of personal mythology to express what he deeply felt. We may not agree with what he thought about organized religion and social restrictions (he was against both), but we keep on with him. What we are looking for are hints about the ways imagination can soar to creative self-assertion. So highly did he regard imagination that he equated it with the divine.

In our own American past we have the "spirit drawings" of the Shaker sect, in which the graphic form of a design was thought to have been "revealed" as a spiritual manifestation. These drawings are among the most fascinating in our own art history.

We are deeply intrigued by the subject of creative intuition and read everything we can find about it. The difficulty is that knowing Freud's ideas about the oceanic state or reading about Blake's mystic visions does not seem to help us much in becoming more intuitive ourselves. However, all the references we consult do reveal some clues about the intuitive state.

The first thing we gather is that a certain amount of solitude is a prime condition of intuition. Solitude has an elusive quality which flees from jangling telephones and the noise of traffic and clattering tongues. Solitude, a place of stillness in which to hear our own inner stillness speak, should be a simple matter to arrange, but the truth is that it is extremely difficult. Considerable creative doing is required just to manage this one necessary thing. However, it is spiritually worth all the trouble, even if no design emerges as a result of it. It is during meditative quiet that we find what Dr. Rollo May has called "a center of strength within ourselves."[7]

We also learn that to achieve intuitive creativeness one must have an attitude which can only be described by using terms which seem contradictory—relaxed alertness. Alertness suggests tension, or at least attention, whereas relaxation implies the lack of tension. Perhaps the explanation is this: we must be relaxed enough so that all our surface thoughts are absent but alert enough to recognize the full play of the

[7] Rollo May, *Man's Search for Himself,* New York, W. W. Norton, 1953.

deep below-the-surface emotions in activity. I believe that this is what Robert Henri meant when he said that "Art need not be intended." It grows, he says, as a branch from a tree, and the fruit is inevitable.[8]

There is another quality of creative intuition which I have not found mentioned in the literature but which I observed at work in the Africans. They associate intuition with rhythm so to them it is a natural occurrence. They speak of the earth as having a heart beat. When they are disturbed or disorganized or out of sorts—in other words when they are unhappy —a tribal African will say, "My heart does not beat with the earth this day." If the disturbance is serious, the medicine man may be called in. Part of his healing will be done in deep silence but part of it will be accompanied by a drum. The drum is played slowly at first, then gradually accelerated until its rhythm is that of a normal pulse. This pulse rhythm has a long duration; finally, as the healing reaches its completion, the rhythm gains a little on the normal, pulling the patient into crescendo with it. He is then considered to be restored to his normal functioning self, in which intuition seems to have a more important role than reason. I observed many times while I lived in the tribal villages that this was truly so.

My own students are more interested in the intuitive than in any other approach to design.

Here are two things which our Fellowship has found highly helpful in the recovery of intuition: one is writing—trying to capture a mood and trap it in words which make an image that can then be translated into lines and shapes; the other is reading the intuitive poets and permitting their metaphors to evoke meaningful images.

We studied Haiku, the little three-line unfinished verses which are so popular in Japan. The memories and moods of the *listener* complete each Haiku differently and silently.

A proper Japanese Haiku has seventeen syllables, the first line five, the second seven, the third five. We did not count syllables in our own verses, because our intent was only to evoke incomplete but meaning-packed images. Getting the images into word symbols aided us in getting them into color and line and shape. Here are three which were written and then illustrated or rather brought into being through art language by members of the Fellowship:

[8] Robert Henri, *The Art Spirit,* Philadelphia and New York, J. B. Lippincott Company, 1951, p. 44.

The red round sun
hangs ripe in the leaves
of the orange trees.

*　　*　　*

The hail runs across the roof
Chased by the angry wind.
Was it caught?

*　　*　　*

The gnarled fingers of leafless trees
Snatch the driven clouds
from the teeth of a dark wind.

A further benefit of our Haiku project was that the children in the various families began writing Haiku, too. The fun of it caught on in clubs and in housing tracts. We are not through with Haiku and never will be, but hundreds and hundreds have already been written in Orange County, California, and many creative selfhoods have been activated because of it.

In connection with our Haiku experiments we read Eric Fromm's *The Forgotten Language*,[5] to see what he had to say about symbols. We liked his statement that "Symbolic language is a language in which inner experiences, feelings and thoughts are expressed as if they were sensory experiences, events in the outer world."

In our second set of experiments, each of us chose a meaningful word to research in poetry. We are in the midst of this project now, and excitement about it is running high in our group. Our interest in this approach was sparked by what Jacques Maritain has to say about the importance of metaphorical inference which "poetic intuition naturally releases."

We began to wonder how Carl Sandburg found little cat feet for his fog, how Emily Dickinson found a vivid relationship between *hope* and *feathers* when she titled a poem *Hope is the Thing with Feathers*. We became highly interested in metaphors. Poets have always known the usefulness of the metaphor, but artists have not always known this. Poets use metaphor to reveal a point of similarity between things which seem highly diverse. The uniqueness of a good poet is his particular genius with metaphor. Why is this not also the uniqueness of an artist?

[5] Erich Fromm, *The Forgotten Language*, New York, Grove Press, 1951.

Emerson gave us a hint about this a long time ago but we didn't listen very well.

For my own experiment, I chose a word which has meant a great deal to me: wind. Since the wind cannot be seen, the only way I could portray it was by manipulating the abstract elements of design. I would have to choose colors and textures and lines which conveyed the feeling I have about a certain wind in a certain place at a certain time. I read a line from Emily Dickinson, "I think that the root of the wind is water." This line took me back to a storm in the south Atlantic when I was crossing in a small ship that was quite unsuited for ocean travel. In that storm the wind that lashed the ship with water seemed indeed to have root in the waves. I am now interpreting this in a stitchery, which, of course, will not show the ship or even the waves. I do not want a literal statement. I want a lyrical, imaginative statement. The direction of the yarns and their colors must say what I am recalling through that line of poetry. The lines in the stitchery are rooted at the base and thinning toward the top as their force is spent. I do not know whether this will be a good stitchery or not, and I do not greatly care. What I do care about is that I am growing in design by attempting to do it.

You have a right to ask here, "How will any one know what you are representing?"

The answer is that quite likely no one will. The beholder, if he wishes to give attention to what I have done, may read into it what he will. It is like a Haiku in that it is an unfinished statement (it will be even after I have completed it), and what the beholder finds in it will be whatever he brings to it of his own perceptions and memories and moods. He may not feel the forces of wind and water at all, but if I am able to do a good piece of work he will feel *something;* that is what he will contribute to what my imagination has stated.

Art which has its genesis in the intuition does not appear to have been calculated. It appears to have *grown* in a way natural only to it.

Winifred Roth took a line from another of Emily Dickinson's poems which tells about a bird who came down a walk, drank a dew from a convenient grass, "and then hopped sidewise to the wall to let a beetle pass."[9] In this work (Fig. 39), which is a combination of wood block

9 Emily Dickinson, *The Complete Poems of Emily Dickinson,* ed. by Thomas H. Johnson, Boston, Little, Brown & Co., 1955. Copyright by Harvard College and the trustees of Amherst College.

and etching, we see a creature world hidden in grass and flowers—"convenient" grass and flowers that can grow only in the imagination.

This kind of working is a feeling forward at every step. It is cumulative. There is mutation in the design at every stage of progress. Each event in the material sets up a new fluid situation which acts on the imagination of the artist. Each happening is "convenient" in that it presents itself to be used or rejected by the artist as it happens. One seizes upon the accidents which contribute to the essence.

In our search through books to find clues to the intuitive state we were greatly aided by the ideas of Sir Wentworth D'Arcy Thompson, who wrote *Growth and Form*. In this book he develops the theme of searching for relationships between things which seem to have none. One can read Emerson and several of the philosophers and find the same emphasis on this search. I believe it was Aristotle's idea in the first place; but Hume and Mill, to name only two of the philosophers, thought this search was central to apprehension.

FIG. 39. . . . *and then hopped sidewise to the wall*, print, Winifred Roth. Photo by Lee Payne.

78

We know that all art and most humor is a matter of relationships. Trite, dull art results from using the *expected* relationships at all times. Humor just dies and disappears in expected relationships: It is the valid but unexpected relationship that produces wit. If illuminating analogies can be reached intuitively, then we have something most precious and rare.

The experience I am about to describe did happen to one of our Fellowship exactly as I describe it. She had selected the word "moon" to research. She went to bed one night wondering whether in the unlikely word "stone," chosen at random, she might find some illuminating analogy with "moon." She had not an idea in her head about any possible relationship when she fell asleep. We know that when we sleep the mind does make significant combinations of the unlikely. (Recall your dreams which seemed absurd but probably would not be absurd if you understood them.) When she awoke in the morning, a vivid image was present in her thoughts. Quickly she jotted down the words:

> I can green the barren moon with meadows,
> Pasture it with sheeply-grazing flocks,
> and polish out the craters with tumbled
> stones of thought.

After this delightful happening, pencils and paper pads went on the bedside tables of all the hopeful members of the Fellowship. We were at the glorious business of image-making, which is imagination.

Another member of the fellowship had chosen the word "hands," hoping to find some intuitive relation between her chosen word and the word "cinders." During her sleep she saw clenched fingers, which she recognized as being her own. The fingers were reluctant to open and do the task set for them, which seemed to be a sifting of dreary gray ash. When they finally obeyed, they found a gleaming gem which she recalled having owned in a small locket when she was a child. This dream was an intense experience and remained with her sufficiently after she awoke so she could capture it in words:

> Unlock your clenched fingers, Hand.
> Spread them out to sift the cinders.
> A gleaming gem rests in the finer ash,
> Ruby fire, now concentrate
> of all that flared so widely, wildly once.

We are just beginning in our Fellowship to exteriorize in art materials these intuitively reached analogies. We are trying to keep them from becoming too literal as they go into paint or mosaic or thread. We want them to suggest much, much more than they state. There is nothing of the occult in what we are attempting. There is nothing even strange about it, either, except that it is rather strange that this approach has not been tried more often in art.

In creative subjectivity we escape captivity by all that is dreary and boring and ordinary. We play with whatever strikes us with a peculiar force. It can be a memory, a line of poetry, a word, a little dust-mouse of thought of our own making. These grow through being fondled by the mind. They grow like jinn or geni out of a bottle, and there is an Arabian Nights enchantment about the process. The reward of cultivating creative subjectivity is a rich, unique personal life that is great fun to live. When we try to express this life of ours in an art statement, we have something to say.

Most of our group grew up in cold parts of the country. We spent one evening recalling winter evenings. We talked about the cold parts

Fig. 40. *Hot Stove, Cold Night*, painting, Eunice Ewing. Photo by Lee Payne.

of houses we remembered (the upstairs bedrooms, the basement where we went to bring up apples) and the warm parts of the house (around the heater in an old-fashioned parlor, near the cookstove in the kitchen). We talked about the feeling of strength which came from the black stoves and which colors we might use to "say" warm and cold. Out of this grew an abstract painting by Eunice Ewing, which combines the strength of black structure with the cools of blues and blue-greens, and the radiance of warm oranges and reds (Fig. 40).

It would be futile to ask, "Where is the stove?" It simply isn't there. This is a lyrical not a literal interpretation of the feeling of strength and warmth amid coldness. You would not need a title to know this if you could see the painting in color.

7 Objective Approaches to design

In objective art the design is consciously planned. The resulting art statement tends to be more literal than lyrical, even when the work is nonfigurative. Events or phenomena are treated as *external* happenings.

Some artists and some schools of art are so dedicated to strictly objective art and to planned design that they will admit of no other kind. Other artists and other schools, just as famous, declare that evidence of subjective feeling—inner apprehension—is the only criterion of a work of art. The difference between these two points of view is vocalized in bitter terms. The split is sometimes talked about under the heading of modern versus traditional, but if we look at the evidence these are the wrong labels. To me the quarrel seems as futile as most quarrels are.

Let us look at the question in terms of ourselves. Do we not some

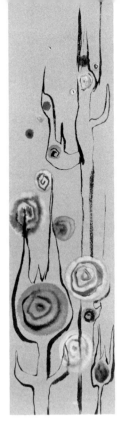

Fig. 41. *Growth Dots*, watercolor, Brenda Wilkinson. Photo by Lee Payne.

times need to plan and organize external events? And do we not also need to live in our dreams and by our intuitions and to see things in symbols of our own manufacture? If a dreamer has no time to dream he is thoroughly frustrated. But if he does have time to dream and fails to rally his objective self to meet the practical demands of daily experience, he will be bumping into corners at every turn. Each of us is both objective and subjective, though by nature we may lean more in one direction than the other. If each of us looks at himself closely he will know where he will find the greater enjoyment. When my closest friends diagnose my personality, they say I am a hopeless romantic, and they say this as though there were no romantics except hopeless ones, though possibly rather endearingly hopeless. The common opinion is that a romantic prefers moonlight to the bright sun of "real" facts. Since I proudly agree that I am a romantic, I want to state what one is. A romantic is a person who wants to reassert imagination and individuality and expression. He believes that a spirit of adventure and wonder

83

reveals the really "real" facts. He doesn't adhere to formal canons, although perhaps he doesn't renounce them either; usually he just doesn't care about them one way or the other. The arbiters of fashion may say that tables or hemlines or hair-dos have to go down this season or that they have to go up, but this isn't a romantic's idea of an adventure. He has adjusted the height of his table so it accords with some feeling he has about the space the table occupies in the room or so it relates to the chair it sits beside, and he will not be a whimling.

A romantic, highly imaginative individual I know fairly well has a sturdy attachment to these things: in poetry, he is devoted to these diverse poets—William Blake, e.e. cummings, Gerard Manley Hopkins, Dylan Thomas, Emily Dickinson, and Shakespeare. The list is not closed. He is willing to add to his shelves any poet—and he will read them all—who has intuitively sought his own images. The poetry of Yeats holds him off a bit because of its mathematical precision and strictness of form. He enjoys the colors which Marianne Moore finds in the world, frog grays and duck-egg greens, but he would like to see more of her images, fresh as they are, depend upon internalization of the external.

In art, he looks at everything with an open mind, even a hopeful mind, hoping to find evidence of some *originality of spirit* to delight his own. He likes the disarming charm he finds in the early American folk artists. He started collecting African sculpture before the museums of this country rescued masks and fetishes from the obscurity of the anthropologists' collections. He would like to have enough money to collect works by Miro, Klee, Rouault, and Chagall. He is not reached by Mondrian—to him Mondrian calculated all the life out of his statements. Our man will have no part in the argument that goes on between figurative and nonfigurative painting. He has seen dull images of recognizable forms, and he has seen dull, nonobjective canvases, turned out as though by formula.

In food, our man likes to experiment with unlikely combinations. He grows herbs. He connives with herbs and sauces and salads and has never been known to follow a recipe precisely.

In furnishings, he feels perfectly at ease with an old Shaker chest at the foot of a bed which has a Danish modern headboard. He can mix periods and styles because he feels the harmonies, the similarities, that hide from a colder eye. He sees that what unites the chest and the headboard is their mutual simplicity, the frank use of materials, the golden gleam that comes from the wood of both teak and pine. There are no "sets" of dishes or suites of furniture or anything else in his house.

People who are fond of our man say he is delightfully different. People who are irritated by him say that he is strange, and they say the word in dark tones. Others say that he is odd. They seem to resent that he conforms so stubbornly to his own tastes. He isn't much worried about people who worry about seeming strange. He knows the decent boundaries of his own deeply-felt polarities. He knows he has not tried to be different for the sake of differentness. He simply has tried to become himself.

This man's opposite number is too well known to need description. He is the efficient executive, even if he does not run a business. Or among women she is the brisk housewife whose engagement book is almost as filled as the executive's. These people make the necessary wheels turn. They plan, and they realize plans. They believe the evidence of their senses and of scientific investigation. Usually they do not want to linger in front of a work of art so as to let the meaning come through to them gradually; they like things more apparent. They are not as interested in hidden rhythms and order as in obvious order.

The Oriental people were wise enough to know that both the subjective and the objective are equally necessary, and they made words and a design symbol for this idea which they called the yin-yang. The idea runs through Chinese folklore, philosophy, medicine, and even magic. Yang is the south or sunny side of the hill, the male, positive, bright, assertive principle. Yin is presumably the north side of the hill, although the dictionary does not state this. It does say, though, that yin is the dreaming, dark, nonassertive principle. (It also says it is the evil principle but I will ignore that.) The yin-yang symbol is a circle halved by a curve, one half dark, the other bright. In this country some courses in dress design ask the student to assess her own personality in terms of yin and yang. I see the words as symbols for the subjective and objective approaches to design.

So far in this book we have stayed fairly close to the north side of the hill. Now we are going south. In my own work, I am pretty far north but I am not sure I would feel at home there if I had not started and stayed a long time in the south. In my teaching I start with objective approaches, and we do not experiment with subjective methods until we are out of the beginning classes. If conscious planning comes first, one has this in his hand when he wishes to work in a more free and intuitive way.

I may wish that the plants of my imagination might always grow in the shadows under the rocky ledge of silent meditation and in the damp leaf mould of dreams and intuitions. But I am not convinced as yet that this plant can come to full flower unless it gets a little sunlight spilling over from the south side of the hill. On the other hand, a work of art can not merely be "good design." If its only merit is lack of offense— that is to say, conformity to the rules of art, it isn't art; it is a barren stereotype.

Right now you have a right to ask a question about the organization of this book. If an awareness of what is "good" design comes first, and if I start my own students out with planned design, why haven't I started *you* out that way? Why did I talk about the subjective first? The reason is that I wanted you to know at the outset that the logically planned and the consciously reasoned, and the techniques acquired through thinking about manipulations of materials and design elements, are not the full glory of art. They are antecedents to more personal attainments. My fear has been that if I were to present these things first, you might be content to stay only with them, not suspecting that they were only the prelude to richer living and deeper experience. When I am teaching a class rather than writing a book, I can be saying this in different ways all along, and the students understand that something larger looms ahead for them to explore.

The danger of over-attention to the reasoned and logical is loss of individuality. The danger of over-emphasis on the intuitive is oddity which can not communicate with those who do not understand a highly personal symbolism. We can be so eager to be clear and concise and "correct" that we end up being calculating. We can also be so eager to penetrate the inner being of ourselves groping for the inner nature of things that we become too amorphous to express the significance we have managed to find in both ourselves and in things. Thus I must conclude that we need to be supple in our attitudes and realize that there are as many paths to beauty as there are to God. Realizing this, it is impossible to be rigid or to think that art can ever be a science. Science, on the other hand, is coming to appreciate in our time the incalculable value of intuition.

I have taken several pages to say what I have said because I think that it is essential to understand these concepts in order successfully to transfigure everyday life through art processes.

THAT'S WHY RULERS ARE MADE

"I can't draw a straight line." This complaint seems more common than the common cold. There isn't any good reason why you need to be able to draw a straight line. That's why rulers are made. If you have a need to draw a circle, buy a compass. If you want algebraic curves, get a French curve.

There is a cleanness, a certain chaste beauty about lines drawn with these mechanical aids. We have some words from Plato concerning this:

I will try to speak of the beauty of shapes, and I do not mean the shapes of living figures, or their imitation in paintings, but I mean straight lines and curves and the shapes made from them, flat or solid, by the lathe, ruler and square. These are not beautiful for any particular reason or purpose, as other things are, but are by their very nature beautiful, and give pleasure of their own.[1]

A fine way to understand some of the innumerable possible interrelationships which can exist among simple geometrical forms is to cut an assortment of them in varied sizes and colors from construction paper. Arrange these forms in a way that pleases you on a background with definite boundaries. You will note that as soon as one small form is placed on the background rectangle a relationship is set up. You will also notice that as soon as you move that small shape the least bit, a new relationship is set up. We add another shape, and the relationships become more complicated. If we are reacting, *feeling* toward these relationships, we will know where to place the shapes to the best advantage and when to cease adding shapes to the arrangement. When the addition of one more component would seem too much, and the elimination of one shape would seem to deprive the design, we have arrived at what, for that particular statement, is the right amount of activity.

There is good entertainment in sitting around a table with family or friends playing a game of geometric arrangements. Each player has

[1] Quoted from Frederick Gore, *Abstract Art,* New York, Crown (no year given).

87

a sheet of construction paper in front of him on which to assemble his creation. In the center of the table are colored circles, triangles, and rectangles. This is the shape-pool from which any player may choose whatever he wishes. Even small children can take part. Many of the Fellowship have told me that the greatest good they receive from our course is the art play they have with their families.

The circles and triangles which you see in Fig. 42, *Shape Game,* could be rearranged in countless ways to produce other statements.

Shape Game was made just for the fun of doing the arrangement, but it is quite likely that if you get an arrangement you really like you will want to *do* something with it. We seem to get an increased satisfaction if we carry out an arrangement in some kind of material. A tribal African will carefully draw a rectangle in the dust with a stick, divide the space into interesting intervals, and spend quite a time filling it in with fascinating motifs. But the moment he is satisfied with it, he will scuff it out and smooth the earth with his great toe. My carriers could never understand why I wanted them to save their dust designs until I could record sketches of them in my notebook. For them, *doing,* not *keeping,* was what was interesting and absorbing. We are more likely to say, "What's it good for? What can I *do* with it?"

F<small>IG</small>. 42.   *Shape Game,* **class experiment. Photo by Arlie Toulouse.**

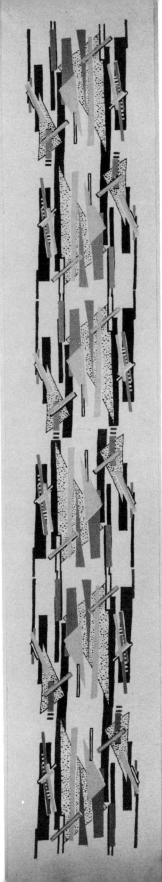

Fig. 43 (*left*). *Extended-Wall Mosaic,* Oakley Parker. Photo by Arlie Toulouse.

Fig. 44 (*right*). *Silk Screen Panel,* Roger Albertson, Iowa State University. Photo by Iowa State Photo Service.

Fig. 45. *Apartment Houses*, stitchery, Donna Read. Photo by Lee Payne.

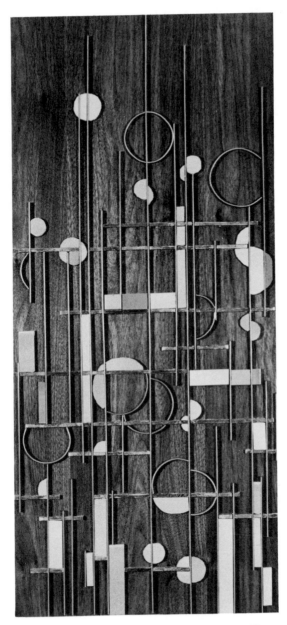

F<small>IG</small>. 46. *Music*, mosaic, Rosita Montgomery. Photo by Lee Payne.

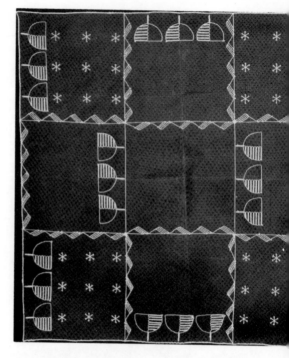

Fig. 47. *Darned Netting*, Katherine Benbrook, Iowa State University. Photo by Iowa State University Photo Service.

The answer is to get it into some appropriate material. The next four pictures are of space games in three different materials. Fig. 43 is a mosaic, Fig. 44 a silk screen, Fig. 45 a stitchery, and Fig. 46 a walnut and brass panel with tile accents.

If we study these four works together, looking from one to the other and back again, we feel a certain common quality which obviously does not come from the media used, since the media are what they have in difference (even though two of them have utilized fabric and two of them tile). What they have in common, I think, is a sort of architectural quality—a built, constructed quality. This brings us to an art word which is good to know—*architectonic*. An architectonic design is one with a structural quality.

Ruler lines were combined with compass lines in Fig. 47, Katherine Benbrook's elegant, orderly design in darned netting.

In Mary Dixon's hooked rug (Fig. 48), a study in grays, we get a hint of what Plato was talking about when he spoke of shapes "by their very nature beautiful."

The tragedy and comedy masks were done as a group project, playing freely with a French curve. They were designed for a Halloween party decoration.

I have a deeper and more ardent reason for championing the geometric approach to design than my own intense pleasure in doing it and in contemplating the result. I have noticed in working with children that their first all-engrossing delight in playing with paint or with clay begins to dim out, usually between the ages of nine and thirteen. They have reached the stage of awareness of realities. They want to draw objects the way they "really look." The paint or the clay no longer has dominion over the child. The child now wants to manage his materials, and when he is not successful at doing so, he decides that he is "not very good at art" and loses interest in it, often for the rest of his life.

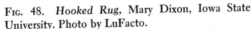

Fig. 48. *Hooked Rug*, Mary Dixon, Iowa State University. Photo by LuFacto.

But if the child, especially if he is a boy, is given a compass and a ruler and encouraged to experiment with them, he will achieve some delightful results. He likes to hear during this age about the discovery of the right angle, how the ancient Egyptian rope-stretchers "corded the temple," how the Greeks evolved geometric puzzles as a means of entertainment.[2] All of this information fits in with his newly-developed interest in facts. It "tides him over" the period when he wants a realism he does not have the drawing ability to achieve.

FRACTURES: THE SUBDIVISIONS OF SPACE

"Come on over with your camera." Merion Seeley of the Fellowship was on the telephone. "I've got the most beautiful dirt you ever saw. It's in the swimming pool."

It was one of those rare days when Southern California is not a pleasant place. A Santana wind was blowing seaward off the desert, stirring the dry soil from all unplanted lots and dropping it again in drifts and swirls.

I hurried over to Merion's house to see the "beautiful dirt." On the top step of the swimming pool, fine brown soil had eddied under the

[2] See Lancelot Hogben, *The Wonderful World of Mathematics,* Garden City, New York, Garden City Books, 1955.

Fig. 49. *French Curve Masks,* students of Esther Dendel. Photo by Arlie Toulouse.

94

Fig. 50. *Natural Fractures*, leaf rubbing, Beverly Nemetz. Photo By Lee Payne.

blue water into a pattern of dark shapes not unlike the markings on the rump of a zebra.

The wind whipped your hair and skirts while I took a photograph of this beautiful fracture of space. What we had were wonderful forms, wind-sculpted within a form (the step of the pool). We studied the slide intently during a meeting of the Fellowship. We sought other natural fractures—old paint curling and peeling on the side of a barn, mud flats baking dry in the desert. Ida and Arlie Toulouse found a piece of ancient linoleum that had peeled and curled on a city dump. It was as beautiful as a painting with petal-like unfurlings where it had split.

Someone owned a Chinese vase on which the crackle glaze showed the same kind of patterning we saw in the sunbaked lake bed.

We talked about the reasons we found these fracturings of surfaces so pleasant to contemplate. It seemed to us that the vital, engrossing thing about natural fractures is that they record evidence of change—growth or contraction; they speak to us of tension, release from tension, and of movement. Growing things in nature are fragmented in a natural way by the growth process. In a leaf the fracturing of the shape by veins is growth evidence. In crackled glaze the fracturing of the surface is the resolution of tension brought about because the glaze has purposely been made too "tight" for the clay beneath it. (If this happens when the ceramist does not intend that it should, the process is called *crazing*.) What is involved is a delicate control of tensions.

We know that persons who are sensitive to line quality can feel the tension set up by two lines that cross; we know, too, that the cross was a powerful symbol long before the advent of Christianity. We are thinking now about the role of tension in design. It would seem that a design without tension is a flabby statement and that one with the right amount of tension has the structural quality we observed in growing leaves.

With these thoughts in mind, we studied stained glass, both the old medieval works and the more recent ones. We were particularly excited by the newly-made windows Marc Chagall had done for a medical center being built in Jerusalem.[3] We studied each one as a whole, and then we made small peep-holes in cardboard which we could move around over the photographs in order to see the rhythm of the leaded lines which separate the colorful shapes.

We also studied the work of Stig Lindberg, the internationally famous Swedish designer whose shapes, broken by lines, give his work its distinctive character.

After studying fractures in the work of other artists and in nature, we tried our hands at the method. Brenda Wilkinson did her experiment with a lion shape, using fine wire to separate the color areas of enamel (Fig. 51). This fellow seems to have a mane like a great flower. Notice that the shapes of the forehead tufts are repeated in the whiskers of his beard, the sprouts of fur coming out of his ears, and the tip of his tail with which he tickles his heel.

"On the first day of Christmas, my true love gave to me . . ." Esther Manker invented forms to capture the symbols of this first section of an old Christmas carol (Fig. 52). She worked in India ink on paper to get a sharply defined fracturing which would reproduce on the newsprint of the newspaper which used her design for their Christmas cover page.

[3] For photographs of the Chagall work see *Look* magazine, Oct. 24, 1961.

FIG. 51.   A *Dahlia of a Dandy*, enamel on copper, Brenda Wilkinson. Photo by Lee Payne.

FIG. 52.   *Partridge in a Pear Tree*, ink, Esther Manker. Photo by Lee Payne.

Shirley Hagman thought that it would be a good experiment to pattern her shapes only slightly and keep the subdivisions of space for the *background*. From this idea grew the linoleum block print we see in Fig. 53.

Lee Hooper found the subject for his experiment (Fig. 54) in the story of *Don Quixote*. This study will emerge as a mosaic.

In a mosaic the grout lines between the tiles not only separate the shapes but develop shapes within shapes. In Fig. 55, Dr. Stevens' mosaic, we can study any one shape, either a light shape or a dark shape, and then be further delighted by the inventiveness of the fractures *within* that shape.

I have the photographs of these experiments spread out in front of me as I write and am delighted with the variety of statement growing out of a single approach to a problem.

Fig. 53 (*left*). *Christmas Birds*, lino-block, Shirley Hagman. Photo by Lee Payne.

Fig. 54 (*right*). *Don Quixote*, mosaic design, Lee Hooper. Photo by Lee Payne.

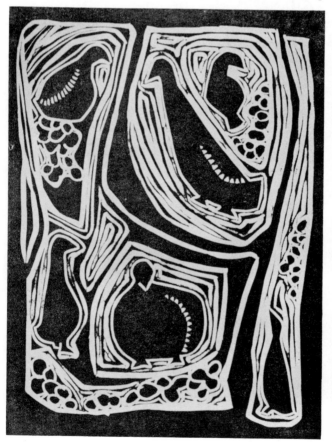

FIG. 55. *Mosaic*. Charles Stevens. Photo by Lee Payne.

DARK CORNER TO DARK CORNER APPROACH

A number of years ago an artist named Kandinsky (and you will enjoy knowing a great many things about *him*), made a little masterpiece which he called *"Lightly Touching."* In this composition, subtly varied triangles in darks against a light background touch at the corners. The dark shapes are so delicately balanced that if one were to shift even a trifle, the whole structure would collapse. This composition has been reproduced over and over. In studying it, designers saw at once that Kandinsky had invented a design approach which could be used to good advantage. The darks make a path for the eye to follow throughout the picture area.

I have been thrilled by the comments my students have made after

99

trying this device. "It has taught me a new way to see," one of them said. "I went out for the coffee break, and I looked at that cluster of palm trees on the campus. I realized that my eyes traveled up a brown trunk to the top of the dark fronds, across to the crown of fronds of the next palm, down the trunk of that tree, along the dark earth, and up the third trunk."

"I saw a fence that way," another one explained. "Before today it was just a brown fence. Today I traveled up one board, across the capping to the next board, down that board, across the base board, and back up again. That's a long way to look at a fence. While I was trav-

Fig. 56. *Flight,* mosaic design, Lee Hooper. Photo by Arlie Toulouse.

elling the boards, I saw some wonderful wood grain I had never noticed before."

We learned that this was a way of looking as well as a way of working.

An advantage of this design technique is that it permits beginners to achieve highly professional-looking results. Another advantage is that it enables the designer to balance the darks in his design rather automatically, leaving him free to confront other problems.

When using this technique, one starts by dividing the design area into delightful intervals of space, using either straight or curved lines or both. The divisions of space may in themselves suggest the subject matter. Curved lines seem suitable for bird or water-living forms. In making the design for *Flight* (Fig. 56), for instance, Lee Hooper did not know what the subject matter of his design would be. The rest of the class were using straight lines to divide space; he used curves in order to do something different. The curves in turn suggested the movement of flying birds. Mr. Hooper executed his design in a mosaic which won first place in the big Wichita National Exhibition of Decorative Arts in 1960.

Mr. Hooper's next experiment with this design approach made use of animal forms. We see the delightful results in Fig. 57, a drawing that is still to be done in mosaic.

The second step is to invent the forms to be distributed over the design area. Sylvia Mello planned her design for a kitchen splash board so she selected bottles, bowls, and spoons for her theme. Many more of these were cut from newspaper than she actually used in order to provide some latitude of choice. The newspaper forms were shifted about until the arrangement was pleasing to her. She then drew around the pattern forms with a pencil.

The third step is to do the shading. Beginning anywhere along 'the outer edge, a single form is darkened. As one works the insignificant small forms are disregarded. Bringing dark point to dark point across

Fig. 57. *Raccoons,* mosaic design, Lee Hooper. Photo by Lee Payne.

the entire composition establishes a path of dark. Sometimes difficulties arise because two dark forms run together. In these areas a middle value is introduced. The unshaded areas of paper are the light values. When the shading is completed, the tonality should be studied carefully. If more middle values would seem to improve the design, either light or dark areas can be changed to intermediate.

Imagine the design held aloft with a pointed stick at the middle. Would it hold this precarious balance or would the darks on one side or the other teeter it to a fall?

The final step is to translate the color values to hues. In Sylvia Mello's splash board the darkest values were brown, the middle values rust, and the light values a creamy yellow. She executed the design in mosaic. This technique also lends itself well to appliqué, block print, stencil, and silk screen.

DESIGN THROUGH FOLLOWING STRUCTURE OF POETRY FORMS

The more one learns about design and literature, the more similarities one finds between the two. In both poetry and pattern we find rhythm achieved through repetition, variety through breaks in the regularity. When one runs easily along an iambic pentameter, for example, the sudden appearance of a trochee is a delight, and we are happy to again resume the iamb.

In fitting design motifs to the rhythm pattern and structure of poetry one learns about both design and literature.

One of my students who teaches literature has done selected poems in design motifs and makes a guessing game of them for her students. She indicates the rhyme pattern by changes in color and the deviations in stress by changes in motif. Sonnets, ballads, and roundels all lend themselves to this treatment.

These "poems in pattern" may be executed on anything—providing an allover design is appropriate. I have seen handsome cabinet doors done in mosaic, the pattern having grown from the structure of a favorite poem which is meaningful to all the members of the family.

Try a sonnet on your garden gate! It could be done in paint, in simple relief carving, or in mosaic.

FIG. 58.   *Step One: The Division of Areas into Space Intervals*, Sylvia Mello. Photo by Arlie Toulouse.

FIG. 59.   *Step Two: The Design Motifs Are Cut from Paper*, Sylvia Mello. Photo by Arlie Toulouse.

FIG. 60.   *Step Three: The Insignificant Areas Are Thrown into Larger Ones and the Color Value of Each Area is Established*, Sylvia Mello. Photo by Arlie Toulouse.

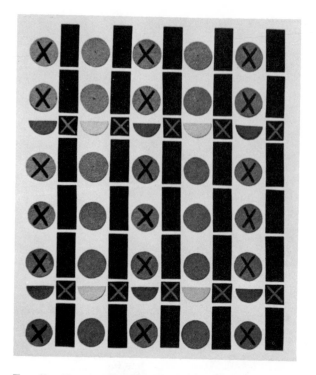

Fig. 61. Two Verses from *The Rubaiyat of Omar Khay-yam* in Design, rhyme pattern a a b a, Student work in Esther Dendel's class. Photo by Arlie Toulouse.

The two designs by Beverly Nemetz, Figs. 62 and 63, are based on nursery rhymes all of us know. They will be carried out in silk screen on throw pillows. We think it would be more fun for you to guess what they are than for us to tell you.

REPETITION WITH VARIATION

Our Fellowship set out to research the import of analogue and metaphor for artists. We found over five hundred quotations by writers, artists, musicians, and poets who had something pertinent to say about likenesses that are obvious, likenesses that are oblique, and the unity to be had from repetition. There is a difference, of course, between re-

FIG. 62. *To Do with a Clock*, verse structure in design, Beverly Nemetz. Photo by Arlie Toulouse.

FIG. 63. *To Do with a Dream*, verse structure in design, Beverly Nemetz. Photo by Arlie Toulouse.

Fig. 64. *Enamel Bowl*, Helen Worrall.

peating and insisting. You will enjoy what Gertrude Stein had to say about that.[4] It is to get away from the monotony of insisting that we try to vary what we repeat, but to do this without losing the unity of the design requires a responsive eye.

In Helen Worrall's beautiful enamel bowl which won the purchase prize in 1958 at the Wichita National Decorative Arts Exhibition (Fig. 64), we see that a responsive eye was at work. As too much variation would have distracted us from the subtle shape of the bowl itself, she has used a repeating motif which rhythmically decreases in size as the

[4] Gertrude Stein, *Lectures in America,* Boston, Beacon, 1935.

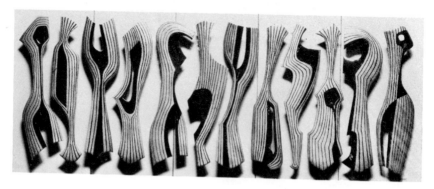

Fig. 65. *Stygian Embers*, enamel panel, Helen Worrall.

circumference of the bowl decreases. This motif never becomes repetitious as she introduces many delicate nuances of change.

Miss Worrall's *Stygian Embers* (Fig. 65) is a flat panel; the figures are raised from the panel and cast shadows. The variety comes from the changing face of the shadows as well as the variation in the raised forms themselves.

In Miss Androsko's tapestry (Fig. 66), we have change of color, change of tone, change of shape, change of direction—all themes played on one motif. Part of the fascination of such a design is that it invites us to analyze for ourselves the variations that have been made.

In the section on Form, later on in this chapter, we discuss a simple shape of a cat, freely cut from newspaper. Almost anyone can cut a good shape if he cuts enough of them, and one seldom goes wrong in

FIG. 66. *Tapestry*, Rita Androsko. Photo by Arlie Toulouse.

FIG. 67. *Six Out of Seven*, mosaic design, Rita Myers. Photo by Arlie Toulouse.

design if one repeats a good shape, introducing enough variation so the motif never becomes monotonous. That is what has been done with the cat shape in Fig. 67.

Brenda Wilkinson started with a single figure of a hooded monk when she began her enamel panels (Fig. 68). She varied the height, the gesture, the position of each figure, and the spacing between the repeated figures.

The Guatemalan and Peruvian peoples are masters at using repetition with enormous variety. Study the Guatemalan hanging in Fig. 69 and try to list all the ways in which variety has been achieved.

DESIGN THROUGH LIMITATION

The approach of design-through-limitation is a variant of the scribble. Instead of making a continuous free-flowing line, one decides beforehand to limit one's means. One gives oneself a definite number of components with which to work. These components may be simply one shape and one line, or, if one wishes more to work with, one may choose, for example, three shapes and five lines. It is good to work

FIG. 68. *Enamel Panel,* Brenda Wilkinson. Photo by Lee Payne.

FIG. 69. *Guatemalan Weaving*, from the collection of Mabel Fisher and Edna
O'Bryan, Iowa State University. Photo by Arlie Toulouse.

Fig. 70. *One Line—One Shape*, bowl design, Robert Collins. Photo by Lee Payne.

rapidly, filling page after page of a sketch book to see how many different things evolve.

In Fig. 70 Bob Collins limited himself to one shape and one line to arrive at a design for a mosaic bowl.

In the insignia for the Idyllwild Arts Foundation, Fig. 71, the design component is limited to one continuous line.

A single line design, or one using line in broken segments, lends itself especially to sewing machine stitchery in which coarse, decorative, colored thread is placed on a bobbin and secured along the design lines by the usual locking action of the needle. This is also a good design technique for darning net and patterning pottery with incised lines. (The first man, according to the African story, patterned his mud walls with incised lines and tribal women still pattern their clay pots with these lines.)

Having first marked off the area whose space is to be divided, one starts at an edge with a line which flows continuously as one directs it. This kind of designing is most successful when the paper is smooth (ordinary shelf paper does very well) and the drawing instrument glides easily. A felt-nib pen is a good instrument for this. This kind of designing differs from the doodle or scribble in that one does some

Fig. 71. *Insignia, Idyllwild Arts Foundation.* Photo by Arlie Toulouse.

Fig. 72. *Labyrinth*, stitchery, Edna O'Bryan, Iowa State University.

Fɪɢ. 73. Place Mat Design for Sewing Machine, Edna O'Bryan, Iowa State University.

casual calculating of space as the line moves forward. The aesthetic pleasure comes from the continuously flowing line and the success of the spacial division.

DESIGN WITH STICK FIGURES

One has only to look at the lively and whimsical stick figures drawn by Paul Klee to realize how delightful and expressive these can be. Humor, action, communication—all are achieved in less-than-skeletal drawings.

After studying Klee's work, our Orange Coast College students tried their hands at drawing stick figures. Although we did not achieve any with the wit of Klee's, we had a good design experience from it. In the design reproduced in Fig. 74, planned for the headboard in a child's room, each figure was drawn by a different member of the class.

Working in a similar way in her Applied Art Class at Iowa State University, Cynthia Thiessen did her stick figures in a block print on fabric. The result is shown in Fig. 75.

FIG. 74. Headboard Design, author's Orange Coast College Adult Education Class.

FIG. 75. *Recess*, blockprint, Cynthia Thiessen. Photo by Arlie Toulouse.

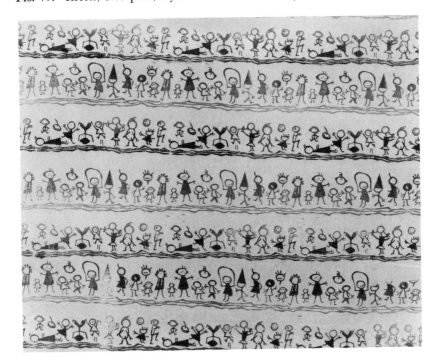

Fig. 76. Basketmaker Indian Fetish, from the collection of Mr. and Mrs. Jo Dendel. Photo by Arlie Toulouse.

MANIPULATION OF THE PLASTIC ELEMENTS OF DESIGN

The plastic elements of design are points (or dots), lines, shapes (or forms), colors, and textures all of which operate in space. They are called plastic because they are formable.

We may think of these as the ingredients of a recipe—they may be combined in endless ways to produce endless results. They are the artist's means of statement. We have been working with them in all the approaches to design which have been suggested so far. What we propose to do now is to manipulate them to see what they can express.

POINTS

Strictly speaking a point is without dimension, but in actual art practice we use points or dots or "spots" of specific sizes.

114

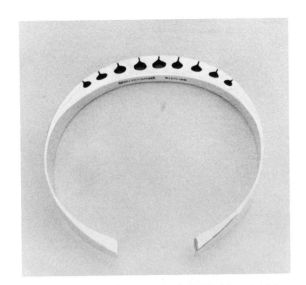

FIG. 77. *Pierced Points,*
bracelet, John Dickerhoff.

FIG. 78. *Point Effect in*
Nature, water-bored beach
rock. Photo by Arlie Tou-
louse.

FIG. 79. *Point Effect in*
Design, cuff links, Bettylou
McCurdy. Photo by Arlie
Toulouse.

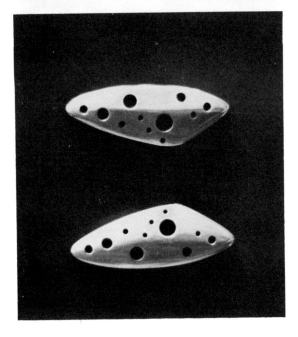

FIG. 80. *Animal*, modeled clay, Adolf Odorfer. Photo by Arlie Toulouse.

FIG. 81. *Points with Lines*, pin, cloisonné enameled on silver, Helen Worrall. (Notice the sensitive distribution of points and spacing of lines.) Photo by Arlie Toulouse.

FIG. 82. *Jug-Eared Cat*, pottery, Mary Pottenger. Photo by Arlie Toulouse.

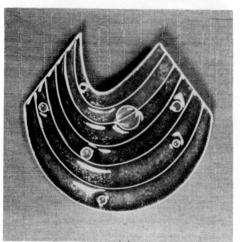

One dark round spot on a white background expresses itself differently in each new location. It may seem to be rising, to be falling, to be moving toward either edge of the frame. Not only does the spot or dot seem to be in different activity in each new location but the background itself changes. It may seem to be hanging or suspended when secured by the dot at the top, to be teetering in uneasy balance when the dot is at the bottom center, or to be pulled to one side when the "weight" of the dark point is there.

Add more dots and you will discover that there is activity among them—collisions, tensions, attractions—all deriving from the way they are placed. Large circles or dots can seem to be "devouring" small ones, small ones can seem to be emerging from large ones. Circles can seem to be "chasing" others, supporting others in delicate balance, rolling like marbles.

It is fascinating to see such things happen as you move the spots about. It is better for you to cut a heap of various-sized circles from paper and have a private, visual party with them than for these effects to be pictured here and labeled. The circle party would not be a surprise party if you knew in advance all that might happen.

As you manipulate the spots you are almost certain to discover that they have a hypnotic quality. Recent experiments dealing with the relationship between visual perception and air safety indicate that circles are not the best form for dials on the instrument board of a plane because of their hypnotic effect. Effort is required to force the eye to quit an emphatic circle and move on to other areas, which is not the case with verticals. One continuous glance can sweep a long rectangular panel. If all the indicating needles are vertical when everything is as it should be, one off-vertical when something is amiss is immediately comprehended.

Dots and dots-within-circles are found so often in primitive design as to suggest that these are the most vigorous and compelling motifs man could invent for magical purpose.

In nature we find prolific examples of points or dots: the grouped points of clusters of berries, the string-of-beads point effect of successive dots in partly developed buds on a stem, the "eye" or target-point of spots on a butterfly's wings.

Helen Worrall used two of the design elements, lines and points, in making the cloisonné enamel-on-silver pin shown in Fig. 81.

In her *Jug-eared Cat* (Fig. 82) Mary Pottenger used the same design elements as Miss Worrall—points and lines. A study of this handsome piece of jewelry and the amusing cat will show the wide range of effects possible in combining point and line to make a pattern. At first glance these two compositions may seem to have nothing in common. Only when you begin to analyze the elements of design do you begin to recognize the similarities.

Before looking at our group's summary of the variations they made using dots or spots, study the play on dots in the watercolor and ink composition by Beverly Nemetz (Fig. 83), and see how many variations you can find in her composition which grew from our "dot problem."

Linoleum is an easy material to carve, and you may want to try your hand at variations of the dot theme by making a block for printing textiles as Dale Hallberg did in the linoleum block photographed in Fig. 84. Most of our Fellowship experiments were made by direct printing with a cut potato dipped into tempera paint. These carved potato dots are practical for printing notepaper; the linoleum cuts are more practical for textiles.

FIG. 83. *Play on Dots*, Beverly Nemetz. Photo by Lee Payne.

FIG. 84. *Play on Dots*, linoleum blockprint by Dale Hallberg. Photo by Arlie Toulouse.

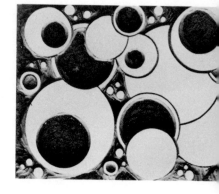

Summary of what can be done with dots

The dot or spot is the simplest element of design. If you understand the possibilities of the dot, you will not only make better designs, but you will also get more pleasure out of washing dishes because soap bubbles are modified dots. You will get more than gastronomic pleasure out of Swiss cheese. You will have a better understanding of Joan Miro's paintings. You will understand why much of the beauty of that famous Byzantine mosaic of the Empress Theodora in Ravenna comes from the "string-of-pearls" effect of the circles or dots.

In order to understand the potentials of the dot in design we need to *experiment* with it and find out for ourselves just how many different things can be done with this simple but powerful little element. Our Fellowship carried out such experiments by printing directly with sliced potatoes and other common objects such as bottle caps, can lids, and round fruits and vegetables. Our first experiment was to try to balance the dots so that if any one were removed, the whole structure would seem to collapse. This taught us a great deal about *balance*.

We then tried to see how much variety could be gotten out of dots. Listing our experiments, we came up with this inventory of possibilities:

1. Vary the size.
2. Vary the spacing between dots.
3. Vary the arrangement of the dots.
4. Fracture the dot by interior divisions.
5. Pattern the dots. (The Japanese have thought of hundreds of ways.)
6. "Ghost" the dots with shadow-like parts of them.
7. Do "line over mass," using a solid circle as the mass.
8. Make the space around the dots brighter or darker than the dots (use of the negative space).
9. Divide the area of the dot and use value reversal in the halves (figure-ground reversal).
10. Dent the dots (study in pressures—interior and exterior).
11. Overlap the dots, using transparencies.
12. Segment the circles and rearrange the segments.
13. Cluster the dots (molecule effect) to study attraction and repulsion of forms.
14. Serrate the edges of the dots.

15. Let the background color or value move into the dots. (In the Lascaux caves the background color of the walls moves into the shapes drawn on the walls.)
16. Scatter the dots and connect them with a line as your eye tends to connect them (study in eye-movement over a surface).
17. Pick up the want-ad page of any daily paper. Make a dot with a felt-tip pencil over every number seven you can find on the page. Use these dots as an image-forming "doodle."

We have not begun to exhaust what can be done with a dot. Number eighteen should be "invent some exercise of your own."

LINES

Lines have various functions. They divide space, they bound forms, they set up movement, they subdivide areas.

In using line to divide space our concern is to set up interesting intervals. When space is equally divided the mind grasps that fact at once. Having comprehended what is to be seen, our attention leaves the subject; there is no reason to look further. On the other hand, if the mind must function to establish the relationship of one space to another, it is entertained by the problem. In designing the linen cloth she wove (Fig. 85), Nell Parker tried many spatial divisions, working with a ruler on graph paper, before she decided on the one she used.

In John Dickerhoff's bracelet (Fig. 86) which was awarded first prize in jewelry at the Wichita Art Association's National Exhibition of Decorative Arts in 1957, we notice that the broad thin section at the back provides the necessary spring for opening and closing as well as giving us the aesthetic pleasure of observing the opposites, thick and thin, in relation to one another. Not only is the line of the bracelet lovely but the cut lines are beautifully spaced.

Lines which extend vertically from boundary to boundary of the frame seem to be neither rising nor falling, because the bounding edge arrests the action in both directions. The eye follows a line up to the top of the frame, then moves horizontally along the frame until another line is provided to take it down again into the design area. Shorter lines in a stair-step arrangement placed near a longer line help to give it an assist in directional movement. Near the top of the design area they boost the rising effect, near the bottom they help "pull down."

FIG. 85. *Space Division with Stripes,* linen cloth, woven by Nell Parker. Photo by Arlie Toulouse.

FIG. 86. *Space Division with Cut Lines,* bracelet, first prize jewelry, Wichita Art Assoc. John Dickerhoff.

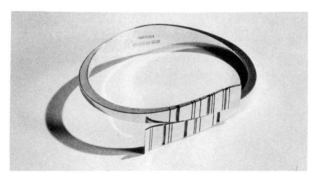

Fig. 87.   *Trees*, silk screen, Sally Kessler. Photo by Arlie Toulouse.

Fig. 88.   *Bent Line*, pin, John Dickerhoff. Photo by Lee Payne.

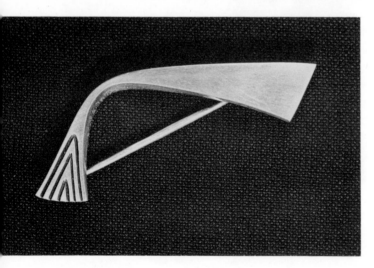

Curved lines are most effective when set against a straight line so the eye can gauge the extent of the curve. In nature we understand the curve of a leaf by its divergence from the straight line of the midrib. If we were given to rules, we would say that every curved design needs a straight line as a point of reference. Designs which are all curves get squiggly. They suggest fish worms or the visceral regions.

What makes a curve beautiful? My students have spent many hours discussing that question. I believe they have arrived at part of the answer. "A curve," said one of them, "is beautiful when it expresses the intent of the person who drew it."

There is a great deal said in that sentence. It implies the power inherent in line-language. Some words are more beautiful to say than other words but, excepting the one-word ejaculation which makes sense of itself, words are expressive only in context with other words. Try, for instance, saying aloud these words from Psalm 137:

We hanged our harps on the willows in the midst thereof.

There is much poetry and lilt in *we hanged our harps,* but any of these words pronounced by itself seems almost startling in its harshness. The same seems true of lines: they are beautiful as they fulfill their function in joint effect.

We enjoy variety in line as in anything else. In her silk screen textile, *Trees* (Fig. 87), Miss Sally Kessler, of the Nonah Craft Center in Franklin, North Carolina, has contrasted thin lines to thick, curved lines to straight ones.

In addition to straight lines and curved lines there are bent lines, which often combine what we enjoy in both straight and curved. A bent line is a curve which is straight in part of its length. In John Dickerhoff's pin (Fig. 88), we see how the bent line combines the grace of a curve with the sturdy strength of a straight line.

We live our lives surrounded by lines. As soon as we become aware of them, we enjoy them keenly, but we do not enjoy them fully until we begin to manipulate them to make a pattern of our own. One of the forms of art that depends the most on a skillful manipulation of line is drawing.

The average art-*un*trained person tends to regard an artist as one who can draw. It would be more accurate to say that an artist is someone who can invent forms and arrange them in a communicative way. Many an individual can sketch a fairly accurate representation of an object but he may have no idea how to relate this to the background, or to the frame, or to other objects in his composition. Others who do not draw with any great skill are able to assemble and compose forms which have great impact.

Sketching, as a practice in observation, is valuable and not to be minimized. However, the artist should not get so carried away with trying to make a photo-like depiction of an object that he neglects composition and spatial arrangement. There really is no point in drawing an object if all one wants to achieve is the closest possible naturalistic imitation. That can be done much more quickly with a camera. Ideally the artist should observe closely, react to the subject, and then express what the object has communicated to him in his drawing.

Drawing should not be an exercise in cleverness but an exercise in selection, in arrangement, in organization, in expression, in interpretation. A drawing should say something, although not necessarily something literal or even anything that can be reduced to words. The language of drawing is a graphic language, not a spoken one. But it is a language we can learn by trying to do creative drawing ourselves and by looking at great drawings done by others.

A unique book, *Modern Prints and Drawings*,[5] has between its covers a range of drawings (and prints) beginning with David and Goya, wonderfully selected by Paul Sachs. As we go slowly through the book, letting each drawing convey to us what we are capable of receiving from it, we are glad that there is no extra stimulant from color. In the blacks and whites and tones are richness and excitement aplenty.

A friend of ours who collects drawings likes them so much that he gave up golf, a country club membership, and smoking in order to afford them. He began buying drawings instead of paintings because he could get drawings of quality for less money. Today, when he could afford paintings, he still buys drawings because he has become so sensitive to line and form that he *prefers* drawings.

It is my considered opinion that one can be taught a few basic principles of drawing but actually no one "can be taught" how to draw. When one has something to express, one will manage the drawing after experiment and patient retrying. Drawing seems more a matter of will, patience, keen observation, and practice than of talent.

[5] *Modern Prints and Drawings,* selected by Paul Sachs, New York, Alfred A. Knopf, 1954.

Fig. 89. *Skin Diver's View*, monoprint, Milo Young. Photo by Arlie Toulouse.

Many laymen suspect that distortion is the result of an inability to draw. While in many cases this is true, the valid reason for distortion is to intensify the statement. An African will draw a crocodile with enormous jaws and a huge tail. The legs are mere matchsticks and the middle section, the body, amounts to almost nothing. If you ask him about this, he will assume you are ignorant about crocodiles, not that he is ignorant about drawing.

"That crocodile can cut a man's leg off in one bite," he will explain. "With the tail he can cut a canoe in two with one hit. Then he will eat the person in the canoe. The crocodile doesn't hurt you with his legs. *They don't have to be big*. And when a person is inside the crocodile, he doesn't care any more so the middle doesn't have to be big."

It is a natural thing for an African to emphasize what is important. He would consider it pointless to strive for verisimilitude. When he draws, the drawing *says something*.

Monoprint is a method of working which combines features of the inked surface with drawing. An example by Milo Young, Fig. 89, is included here. Milo is a student at the Los Angeles County Art Institute. During the summer months he earns his living skin-diving for abalone and other under-water creatures. Down in the ocean depths he encounters a whole new wondrous world of colors and forms. He makes the transformation of nature into art by doing personal interpretations in the medium of monoprint. In making a monoprint the face of the paper is in contact with an inked surface while the drawing is freely done on the back of the paper. The pressure of the pencil on the paper picks up the ink in contact with the paper. Sometimes Milo prepares the paper with flat color areas before placing it in contact with the ink.

"What I attempt to achieve," he says, "is a linear interpretation with a feeling for spatial arrangements which produce a core movement in composition."

Trying to draw what one feels about a selected subject is highly rewarding. One learns to see and observe closely things he has never noticed before. This heightened awareness brings a heightened sense of life.

FORMS

Form is, I think, the most interesting and important of all the plastic elements and the one which presents the most challenge to the designer. The patterns or shapes in painting and drawing are two-dimensional forms; furniture, sculpture, bowls, buildings are three-dimensional forms.

Thousands of men in this country have power tools. Usually they manage these tools well. But most of them feel lost without a model or paper pattern or blueprint to follow. As a result they *copy* form more often than they *invent* form. Often the copied production does not fit the place it will be used, either in scale or in spirit.

One does not learn all about form by reading a few pages of a book. But a few guides can be given:

Ask any high school boy what make and model of car has just passed. If he had even a brief glimpse of it, he probably can tell you. Boys and most men are intensely *aware* of the subtle nuances of form in cars. They have definite opinions about this, usually without being aware that they are making *aesthetic* judgments. If the same intense awareness that is lavished on cars and boats were given to chairs and bowls, our homes would be more handsomely furnished.

First of all, then, one must be aware of the forms that exist around one. Collect water-tumbled pebbles from the bed of a stream, clutch them in your palm, slide your fingers over the surfaces—surfaces so smooth they sometimes feel waxed. One of these stones, when you have looked at it long enough and fondled it sufficiently, will have communicated through your senses a new feeling for beautiful form. You will have memorized the feel of a beautiful shape. Then try looking at a chair, not seeing it as a chair for the moment but as a form in space. Regard the handles of tools in the same way. Many of them are as beautiful as sculpture.

Secondly, be aware of utility—if the form is to serve a function. Furniture, for example, is made for a purpose. The purpose of a chair is to hold a seated human in comfort. We all have seen chairs which may be capable of holding the weight of a human, but which seem too flimsy to perform their function; so if sit in them we must, we do not settle into the chair but perch gingerly on the edge awaiting the expected collapse. More common is the chair which is embarrassingly ugly but so comfortable that the man of the house flatly refuses to let it go into discard. This kind of furniture fulfills its physical function in a room but not its aesthetic function. Over-scaling is the common fault of furniture produced in the home workshop.

Thirdly, be aware of proportion. In our eagerness to have the object "hold up" we tend to overbuild. We owe a debt of gratitude to the Scandinavian craftsmen for their leadership in solving this problem. Some of their chairs are as beautiful as sculpture, in addition to being comfortable and well-crafted.

In our own home we built one couch ten feet long under book shelves which reach to the drop ceiling or soffit. This wall is opposite the fireplace. Our problem was to make the book wall balance the fireplace wall in visual "weight" without getting a bulky piece of furniture. Our solution was to cantilever the seat-section of the couch, bringing it into harmony with the cantilevered hearth opposite. We made perhaps a dozen mock-ups out of cheap plyscore in order to establish the most comfortable angle of seat to back before we built the actual furniture from mahogany.

In two-dimensional design, the thorniest problem for beginners is to invent the forms to be used.

"I can't draw," people wail. "How can I get my design?"

By cutting forms from newspaper with scissors, those who think they can't draw often get better forms than those who do draw. The beginner in drawing tends to make fussy, nervous little patterns bristling with surface details which have nothing to do with essential form or structure. It is difficult to make fussy forms with scissors. The long blades tend to produce slow curves and graceful shapes. Newspaper is expendable, which contributes to a relaxed and experimental attitude. Cut forms have the added advantage of being movable so they can be shifted about freely on a background, and space relations can be perceived. If you go about this in a relaxed spirit, you are almost certain to get some fine forms.

In Fig. 90 we have a fine cat, freely cut from newspaper. We will meet Rita's cat again later on when we consider composition. For the moment let us regard it simply as an isolated form and consider its virtues.

One notices first, I think, the rhythmic quality of the bounding edge. The curve on the left side is balanced by a different but similar curve on the right. The quicker curve of the head portion and the slower curve of the tail give variety.

FIG. 90. *Cat,* freely cut paper shape, Rita Myers. Photo by Arlie Toulouse.

Concavities balanced by convexities are everywhere in nature. The rounded cap of the knee is balanced by the hollow behind the knee. In our cat we see concavity balanced by convexity. This principle is the basis of our estimate of a bowl as form, of a chair, of sculpture, too.

Compositions of form may be classified as *open* or *closed*. In an open design the pattern seems to extend beyond the bounding edge. The frame "crops" the pattern. If the design forms are sharply different from the background, the shapes may direct the eye out of the picture in too forceful a manner; therefore the form must be muted where it leaves the boundary, and, as this requires considerable skill, the beginner may have difficulty doing it. In this type of composition it is also important that a form which takes the eye away from the design area be balanced by another form which brings the eye of the beholder back into the picture.

In closed composition all of the movement set up by the pattern is contained within the bounding edges. Sometimes in closed design the form or forms actually touch the bounding edge and seem like braces or struts against the frame. In Helen Worrall's pendant (Fig. 91) the bounding edge is the heavily oxidized silver off-round background. The design form, which seems braced against the bounding edge, is a cast gold five-pointed irregular star. The center of interest, which is not dead center, is the pearl. The five-pointed star has a long and fascinating history as a symbol. It has been the symbol of the Virgin and was once considered to have enough power within itself to stand off the devil. It is one of the most usable forms for design as it lends itself to many variations.

The forms we wish to have exert themselves, that is, the forms which make up the pattern, are the *positive* forms. When these positive forms are placed on a background, the areas around them become negative shapes, and these are almost as important as the positive ones.

In two-dimensional design we try to integrate background and foreground in order to avoid violating the design surface. We do not want visual "holes" in the picture plane or in the wall on which our stitchery or mosaic or block print will be hung.

When the background color appears in small amounts in the positive forms, and the design colors appear in the negative spaces we achieve this integration—the two "weave" together. In Mildred Gibson's design (Fig. 92), which would be suitable for appliqué, blockprint, silk screen, or mosaic, we see a fine example of this interplay of foreground and background.

A profitable way to study positive and negative form is to place a sheet of tracing paper over a reproduction of a masterpiece which has withstood the winnowing of time. Trace the broad outline of the forms lightly in order not to damage the print beneath. Then shade the darkest areas dark, the medium-dark areas a medium value, and leave the paper untouched where the painting was light. You lose the details of subject matter which might distract by doing this and can study the forms for their plastic value. El Greco's work lends itself particularly well to this exercise. In any good painting both the positive and negative forms will emerge as interesting related shapes that build into a rhythmic unity.

You can transfer these shapes to construction paper of three values, cut them out with scissors, and try making your own arrangement with them. You will find it difficult but highly interesting to improve on the arrangement of forms of an old master.

Forms set up motion by the manner of their distribution, as we have already mentioned when discussing the manipulation of geometric forms. But they also have *tensions* within themselves. If one could take a quick close-up photograph of a football at the moment it is kicked, the photo would reveal a surprising indentation in the usually symmetrical form. Remembering the football while drawing free-form patterns helps one to understand the seeming pressure from without on concavities of form, the seeming pressures from within on convexities of form. There should be a felt balance of pressures or tensions in irregular form. This is true not because it is a "rule" that someone "made up" but because it is a physical fact felt within our own bodies if we are sufficiently aware to be sensitive to our surroundings.

TEXTURE

The textures of things we make have in them a permanent record of the doing.

We look at a length of handwoven fabric. Even though the weaver was an excellent craftsman and handled the loom well, we probably will discover some variations in the compactness of the threads (this is part of the quality of handwoven cloth) and can estimate where one session

Fig. 91. *Braced Form*, pendant, Helen Worrall.

Fig. 92. *Flower Forms*, Mildred Gibson. Photo by Arlie Toulouse.

at the loom began and another ended. We see that in some areas the beater was pulled forward with a little more energy than in other areas. Noticing this we think, "the weaver woke early that morning and 'walked strong' to his loom. His strength shows here."

By seeing the record left in the material we can feel we are with the worker at his work. In a wood engraving we can tell where the tool was pushed with vigor, where it barely skimmed the surface, where harder particles of wood resisted the push of the tool. In the little ridges that appear from pressures on the moist clay of a wheel-thrown pot, in the barely perceptible grooves on a lathe-turned bowl, in the loops of yarn on a stitchery, in the grout lines that run between the tiles of a mosaic, there are the "tracks of strength" left by the worker's hand or by the tool, which, when rightly used is a hand-extension. The line quality of a pushed pen may tell us more about a friend's state of mind than the words he uses in his letter to us. The line flows with more than usual fluency, or it is constricted and sometimes broken, and the jabbed paper records distraction or frustration.

Machine products may and often do have texture—the loops in a shag rug, for instance—but machined products have in their textures the automatic, unvarying machine tempo, not the life-tempo, not the rise and slackening of energy, not the work-pace of the craftsman. It is this life record of the doer that gives the handcrafted article its greatest appeal and value.

I look at one of the country cloths I brought from Africa. There are many things that I could notice about this cloth—the beautiful division of space, the sensitive division of light and dark, the permanence of the jungle-grown indigo dye. I might recall the night I slept by a raging river too flood-swollen to cross when this cloth was my only covering. But as I look at the cloth I see a knot, a lump of thread snarled in the spinning. Immediately my mind jumps to the scene of a village compound. Many women are seated on straw mats in the shade of an enormous silk-cotton tree. The women are spinning cotton with little clay tops that whirl in giddy profusion. Suddenly a baby cries from inside a mud house. One of the women tenses into alert listening. Her spinning top is jerked to a halt. The thread snarls in a hard little lump. The baby cries again. Yes, it is her baby. She rushes inside the house, leaving the stilled top on its side.

Now I was not in the village when the thread was spun for my particular length of country cloth. I did not see any of the above happen in just exactly this manner, although I saw similar scenes. But now, at this moment, sitting in my California home, I look at the lump of thread in the cloth and I am sitting with the women under that silk-cotton tree and watching the little black clay top jerked to a halt. It may not have been a baby's cry that caused this imperfection. Perhaps it was the smell of rice scorching over a cooking fire. It does not matter. What does matter is that this little snarl of thread speaks with eloquence of a work-rhythm halted, then resumed, and that I can participate in this small drama a continent and an ocean and several years removed.

Many of us own quilts that have "come down in the family." We may know that great-grandmother did all the piecing and quilting of a particular quilt. We look carefully at the tiny stitches which at first glance seem uniformly small and immaculate. But closer study tells us that great grandmother, for all her patience, had working periods less placid than others. In some certain spot there is an uncertainty of procedure, and we know that on that day things were "at sixes or sevens," and more than likely grandmother stuck her finger and frowned and "had to get hold of herself" to even out whatever troubled her. So we travel back in time through this minute change of texture and are for a moment in a generation and a way of life that was done and gone before our own birth.

We enjoy the letters of Van Gogh because through his words we sit beside him before he began his work. It is not that his drawings need words to accompany them; they are strong statements which communicate directly. We look at the vigorous pen strokes, the cross-hatchings, the places where the pen paused while the ink continued to flow. Through these textures we are "with" Van Gogh while he worked. The letters are additional booty. In them we learn what Van Gogh felt toward the subject and how he looked at it, what details he observed as significant *before* he started to draw. Through the letters we are with Van Gogh during the conceptual phase.

The nuances of texture which are part of all hand-done things are most discernible to those who are craftsmen themselves. It is worthwhile to be a doer if only for the increased pleasure one is then capable of taking from what other doers have done.

In the seaport towns of the West African coast it is the imported white enamel basin that is the treasured possession, rather than the

Fig. 93. *Visual Texture*, mosaic design, class experiment. Photo by Arlie Toulouse.

Fig. 94. *Tactile Texture*, rug, Mary Jean Stoddard, Professor Mabel Fisher's Class, Iowa State University. Iowa State University Photo Service.

unglazed black clay pot. It is the starch-slick, sleazy trade goods, not the durable country cloth of the looms in the hinterland that eager purchasers rush to the markets to buy. Standards of value are as confused as they were, and sometimes still are, in the United States. Here, however, machined products are beginning to be recognized for what they are, even though there lingers in the memory of many of us a time when we thought "store-bought" was better. We appreciate the great choice, the variety of forms, that machine production makes possible. We appreciate machine-made textures when they do not imitate the hand textures of craft production. The hand-hammered bowl is honored but the machine-dented copper, imitating the hand process, is rejected for the fraud that it is.

Most of us will select and arrange more textures than we will produce with our own work, no matter how ardent we may be in craft production, but the same guides apply to both. What we want is harmony which stops short of monotony. We do not need rules to arrive at this. All we need to do is to make ourselves aware of tactile quality. We then introduce enough variety to stimulate our interest, but we keep enough similarity so that what we assemble seems in unity. In my own home the texture to which all else is keyed is the fireplace wall of stone. We quarried this stone ourselves, prying it out of mountain, rejecting those slabs that seemed over-coarse in grain. The wall is not too rough to slide a hand or a dust cloth over easily but neither is it a smooth surface. Obviously, nubby draperies, a stitchery on burlap, hand-loomed cushion covers, and a mosaic table top are more in keeping with the stone than silk, velvet, or marble. But in the other direction, the direction of smoothness, we have lamps made from the glass spheres used by the Japanese to float their fish nets and hand-rubbed mahogany furniture.

We rightly think of texture as the "feel" of a surface to the hand, but texture is also the "feel" of a surface to the mind. The mind has a tendency to register "seen" surfaces as rough or smooth or broken and to associate these seen qualities with movement, the smooth-appearing surfaces being "still," the agitated surfaces in activity. If we experiment with created textures in design, we soon see how the twist of a stiff brush or other tool can set up a motion quality to be "felt" in the mind rather than "felt" with the hand. The dauber in a shoe polish bottle is good for this kind of experimenting, as are many other articles of common use.

FIG. 95. Wood Engraving, Jo Dendel, decoration for
New Song in a Strange Land by Esther Warner (Hough-
ton-Mifflin). Photo by Arlie Toulouse.

When we have seen how these motion-qualities of texture work,
then we can combine them with form and with color so that all three of
these plastic elements work together in our design.

"Seen" textures and interesting divisions of space were the design
problems which challenged Jo Dendel in his engraving of an African
hut, Fig. 95.

The wadding of clay is one of the oldest methods of making pottery.
The amount of pressure used in the forming process is recorded in the
finished product, and this is the special charm of the technique. The
wads of moist clay are pressed together firmly enough so they will hold
during the firing but not so firmly that they disappear as separate little
entities which are part of a larger entity. In the lamp, shown in Fig.
96, one of a pair made by Mr. and Mrs. Thomas Pickering for their
Lido Isle home, charcoal-colored clay was used. The form was achieved

Fig. 96 (*left*). Wadded Clay Lamp, Mr. and Mrs. Thomas Pickering. Photo by Arlie Toulouse.

Fig. 97 (*right*). Gnarled Root, owned by Mr. and Mrs. Arlie Toulouse. Photo by Arlie Toulouse.

by pressing the wadded clay against the inside of a drain pipe which was slipped off as soon as the clay was leather-firm. The glaze, a dull white matte, was applied over the entire surface, and then scraped off the upper surfaces to expose the clay but was left in the crevices to emphasize their depth.

Just as texture is the record of natural events which occurred during the making of a handcrafted article, so the textures of a tree are an autobiography of its growth. A gnarled root is used as a decorative accent on the adobe fireplace wall of Mr. and Mrs. Arlie Toulouse (Fig. 97). Finding this root, recognizing its beauty, and bringing it home from the forest were art experiences, as is the present constant enjoyment of its texture.

Observe how the pebbly natural texture of seeds was used by Brook Dickerhoff to make a mosaic which she designed herself (Fig. 98).

We have learned a great deal about texture in our Fellowship by

FIG. 98 (*left*). *Seed Textures*, mosaic, Brook Dickerhoff, aged 6. Photo by Lee Payne.

FIG. 99 (*right*). *San Francisco*, graffito, Jeanette Hawkinson. Photo by Lee Payne.

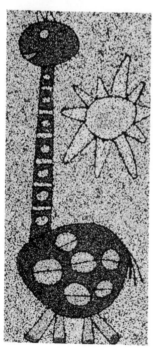

FIG. 100. *Thrust of Spring*, graffito, Beth Willie. Photo by Lee Payne.

experimenting with graffito. Graffito is pattern produced by scratching through a surface layer to reveal different color beneath. We found that using ordinary house paint on tempered masonite gave us an inexpensive set of materials.

Miss Hawkinson divided her area into space intervals and applied each of her three colors three times in the spatial areas. A matte black was then brushed over the entire surface. The under-colors glow in their grooves as the scratching process uncovered them. Fig. 99 reproduces her graffito.

Beth Willie varied the process by spreading each of her three chosen colors over the *entire* area of the masonite. The depth of the scratching determined which of the under layers of color would show (Fig. 100).

COLOR

The greatest obstacle to our study of color is the lack of a precise vocabulary. We read in the advertisements of "shocking pink" or "ice blue" or "hunter green." What do these words mean? Nothing whatever in an exact sense. It is as though a composer tried to write music by indicating sounds as a choo-choo rumble, a pigeon coo, a fire siren shriek, a trickling water splash. A musician writes music with notes which indicate exact sounds and which can be reproduced and recombined. A certain note will indicate the same pitch to a maestro as well as to a piano tuner.

Artists and educators who resist a further and more definite classification of color usually advance the argument that more precision would destroy spontaneity. However, it is a matter of record that precise description of pitch has furthered creativity in music.

Colors are very different things to different people, and this fact adds to the confusion. To those who work with color in lighting, the primary colors, those essential for making all other colors, are red, green, and purple! To the artist or the house painter mixing pigments rather than light, the primary colors are red, blue, and yellow! The psychologist recognizes *four* primary colors—yellow, blue, green, and red! (The reason being that when the eye of the beholder does the mixing of color, green does not seem to be produced by placing yellow next to blue.) We see that before we can say that certain colors are the basic ones from which all others can be made, we must first decide whether we are going to be working in pigment, in light, in the problem of adjacent color, or in a combination of these. For our purpose, we shall consider the primary colors to be *red, blue,* and *yellow.*

Sir Isaac Newton, who is famous for having developed the theory of gravity, was the first to discover that if white light is directed through a prism, all of the colors which compose white light will be broken down into a rainbow band. Although Newton was knighted for his contributions, his work led to controversy and abuse. Three years after presenting his paper to the Royal Society he wrote, "I was so persecuted with discussions arising out of my theory of light that I blamed my own imprudence for parting with so substantial a blessing as my quiet to run after a shadow." [6]

Several color systems have been developed, chief among them the Munsell and the Prang. The Munsell system is the one used and recommended by the U. S. Department of Agriculture and the International Printing Ink Corporation, and it provides the most accurate way we have at present to describe color.

An entire book could be written on color (and many have been) without coming to the end of the subject, because new discoveries are constantly being made. In the present book we wish to take an experi-

[6] *Encyclopaedia Britannica,* Chicago, 1948, Vol. 16, p. 361.

mental approach to color; to place various colors beside one another and observe what happens.

To begin, we need only a few words of terminology so that we can discuss what we do.

COLOR TERMINOLOGY

Spectrum colors: If white light is directed through a prism, all of the colors which compose white light will be broken down into a rainbow band. These spectrum colors are what we mean by *normal* color.

The *attributes* of color are *Hue, Value,* and *Intensity.*

Hue is the name by which we distinguish a color—red, green, yellow, or whatever.

Value is the lightness or darkness of a color. A light value is called a TINT, a dark value a SHADE.

Intensity (or chroma) is the color strength of any hue. When any color is as bright as it is possible for that color to be, it is at full intensity.

Color wheel is made (in the Prang system) by bending the colors of the spectrum into a circle with yellow at the top.

Complementary colors are those directly across from one another on the color wheel.

Related colors are those hues which are close together on the color wheel. They are "blood relatives" in that one color is in all of them. For instance, yellow, yellow-green, and green are all related by the yellow that is in each of them.

Neutral or *grayed colors* are those which have lost some of their intensity by having been mixed with some of the pigment of the complement.

Primary colors are the basic colors required for making other hues. In pigment (although not in light) they are red, blue, and yellow.

Secondary (or binary) COLORS are made by mixing two of the primaries—yellow and blue to make green, red and blue to make purple, red and yellow to make orange.

Tertiary colors are mixtures of secondary colors.

With this vocabulary in mind, we are ready, with a color wheel nearby, to start working with color. The hues on the right hand side of the wheel, the blues and greens, are *cool colors*. Those on the left, the reds and oranges, are the *warm colors*. They not only seem warmer; they actually *are,* a fact which can be registered with a very sensitive instrument.

In order to start thinking in terms of the vocabulary we have just mastered and to become more sensitive to those dimensions in which colors differ, let us select a sample of your favorite color. Ask yourself these questions about it. What is the *hue?* Is it light, medium, or dark in *value?* Is it full *intensity,* half-way to grey? One quarter? Is it a *primary* color? A *secondary?* A *tertiary?*

Having answered these questions, making use of the color terminology, let us start using other colors with your favorite color to form a *color scheme.* The first thing you will notice when you start doing this is that as soon as you introduce a second color, the first one changes in some subtle way and is no longer the color with which you started. This is the great excitement of color work—the relationships between color.

You will notice, too, that some colors seem to advance and others to recede.

As a practice exercise, let us consider a number of different kinds of color schemes built on the favorite color you have selected.

Let us start with a monochromatic color scheme. This is made by using different values or intensities of the *same hue.* It makes a subtle color scheme, especially when low intensity colors are used. Shading from beige to brown, for instance, you have made a monochromatic scheme of grayed color running from light value (beige) to the dark value, brown. Persons who are sensitive to slight and subtle variations in value and intensity find deep, restful satisfaction in contemplating desert landscapes of the kind that abound in southern Utah and many other places in our West. Others whose eyes are neon sign-conditioned find earth hues of low intensity dull and drab, even monotonous. "It is all the same," they say. "There is nothing to see." The fact is that there is much to see but dazzle-fatigued eyes are not conditioned to see what is there.

The kind of color you will want in your own home depends a great deal upon the kind of life you lead. In our home we chose low-keyed monochromatic color. We lead extremely active lives, sometimes talking to several hundred persons in the course of a day. When we enter our living room we want to settle into comfortable chairs and pick up good books. We have our excitement in our work so we do not want color excitation in our home. In the patio, which we see only when passing from the studio to the house, we have a bright mosaic, a "lift" of color on our way to rest.

There are two other kinds of color schemes we can choose; one using related colors, one using complementary colors. Related colors with a neutral make a highly satisfying scheme. Complementary and split-complementary schemes are more difficult to use, as complements "force" one another when adjacent, each making the other seem brighter than it seems alone.

So far in this exercise, we have said nothing about areas or quantities of color. We have merely been looking at various *types* of color schemes. There is a LAW OF COLOR AREAS which holds that the larger the color area, the less intense the color should be, and the smaller the color area, the brighter it may be. Bright colors seem jewel-like and precious when used in small quantities. They assault the eye and tire us when they are used in large areas.

After deciding on your color scheme and upon the size area that each of the colors in the scheme should occupy, the next problem is to decide how you should *distribute* the various colors throughout the composition. A common mistake, especially in mosaics, is to get bright colors in tight little bunches which make spots. Think of your bright colors as thread and think about how you can "darn" them through the composition. Study the works of great painters to see how they have done this. Van Gogh was a great master at distributing color. It is thrilling to note how he threads a tiny line of intense red through the green of his trees. The rhythm of your work will depend as much upon the distribution of bright color as upon your drawing.

A fine way to get *balance* into your work is to *triangulate* color. Select any one of your already chosen colors and place a chip of it at the three tips of an imagined triangle. Do this with all the bright colors in your scheme. As you do this you will discover one of the wonderful properties of color—that repeated bright color circulated about in your design sets up a *sense of movement*.

You have no doubt also noted by now that color has an effect beyond the boundaries of the form that contains it. This is called its "halo" effect. This effect is sometimes increased by carrying bright color under and beyond the bounding edge of the forms within the design.

After you have played with color samples and observed their relationships you will enjoy studying paintings by some of the great colorists of the past. Of particular interest are the Impressionists who, although they lost form in the process, achieved brilliant vibratory effects in their experiments with light and shadow. The Pointillists used the device of placing small dots or dashes of color next to one another so they could be "mixed" by the eye of the beholder. This color technique is especially applicable to mosaic.

You will want to study Cezanne, who *built form with color.* And you will enjoy the *Fauves,* who held that a color exists in its own strength as a plastic element and does not need to give literal description to form.

After playing with color chips and observing how others have used color and to what effect, you may want to spread out samples of colors you plan to use in a composition to give yourself a fair picture of their cumulative effect. When deciding if the colors chosen for a design are appropriate, ask yourself these questions:

1. Is there *one* outstanding color effect? This is the design principle of UNITY. The one effect might be the result of one color in various intensities or values running throughout much of the composition.
2. Is enough *neutral* color used to keep the vivid colors together? Neutrals are "shock absorbers."
3. Are these colors ones that you will enjoy living with for some time? (Colors which are too intense get "worn out." Actually it is our eyes which wear out from too much seeing of vibrant color.)
4. Are these colors suitable for the *use* that is to be made of them? A table that is "overbright" seems to leave the floor. Visually, it does not stay down.
5. Are there enough dark values so the total effect is one of richness? Mosaics, especially, seem to be enriched by dark values. Darks keep a composition from being weak.

If the answer to these questions is "yes," then I think you are ready to start to work, whether your project is a stitchery, a silk screen, a mosaic, a costume, or a pillow for the couch.

SPACE

The elements of design which we have just been considering operate in space, either two- or three-dimensional. Let us consider how this works.

An architect designs with space, the exterior of a building being the boundaries of the space that is enclosed, the interior walls the divisions of the enclosed space. A sculptor, too, works in three-dimensional space, as does the designer of furniture or of pottery.

A flat picture surface is another matter. Here we have two dimensions, length and width, and we have to make some decisions about how much depth will be suggested by what we do to the surface.

A plane is a flat surface with boundaries. When we begin a stitchery, the dimensions of the fabric constitute a plane. When we paint a picture, the canvas is the picture plane. As soon as even one color is added to the canvas, it is no longer strictly two-dimensional because the color will tend to advance if it is an advancing color or recede back of the picture plane if it is a receding color. No composition can be strictly two-dimensional. The third dimension is suggested as soon as color is added. Even texture of a neutral color can suggest the third dimension.

During most of the long history of painting, the illusion of depth was not pushed beyond shallow limits. During the Renaissance, when so-called "scientific" perspective was discovered, many painters carried the new principles to what seems to us today to be excessive lengths. It was much the same situation as when the jig saw first came on the market. Builders were enchanted with what the tool could do, and houses had curlicues and wooden "lace" tacked on at every imaginable spot.

Today we know that one-point perspective, which once seemed a great revolutionary idea, is only one of several ways of manipulating visual space. The Chinese painters open up the "picture box" to the beholder instead of closing it down toward a vanishing point in the imagined distance. Their lines of perspective converge toward the spectator.

Cezanne had another way of treating space. He must have considered that the human eye is capable of moving, the human head capable of being turned, thus further extending the range of vision. His perspective is one of multiple-view. Erle Loran's *Cezanne's Composition* [7] is a book which increases one's capacity to enjoy Cezanne's great pioneering efforts in spatial management.

Today we tend to the belief that the picture plane should be respected

[7] Erle Loran, *Cezanne's Composition,* Berkeley and Los Angeles, University of California Press, 1943.

and that deep depth is a violation of the picture plane. We try to avoid "holes in the wall" from deep simulated distance. We use overlapping planes without feeling any necessity to diminish the size of those in the rear, because we know that overlapped planes are recessive and that as they are raised vertically on the picture surface they seem more so. When we arrange planes in this manner, we are experimenting with them as plastic elements rather than blindly following the laws of one type of perspective.

Similarly, we may want to penetrate through the front plane to depict an object which we know is hidden from actual view by the forward one.

Experiments with overlapping and interpenetrating planes can be carried out with colored cellophanes. We notice as we work with these that as color deepens in the overlapped areas the darker recessive planes seem to push the lighter forward ones to the front.

FIG. 101. *Overlapped Planes*, stitchery, Betty Lou King. Photo by Arlie Toulouse.

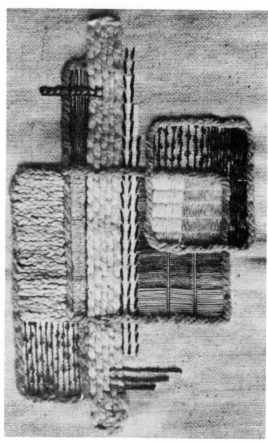

Planes parallel to the picture plane are called *static* because they do not set up any movement, except if they are overlapped, then they appear to move back into depth. Planes with diagonal boundaries are called *dynamic* because they set up movements of thrust and of rotation.

In Betty Lou King's stitchery we see an effective use of overlapped planes operating on a flat surface—the burlap background (Fig. 101).

John Dickerhoff's sculpture gives us a feel of satisfaction and security because of the way the planes are tilted but locked together (Fig. 102).

Dale Hallberg penetrated a solid, and the eye takes its pleasure from entering the solid in the pierced areas and "going around behind" the curved surface (Fig. 103).

Fig. 102 (*left*). *Interlocking Planes*, John Dickerhoff. Photo by Lee Payne.

Fig. 103 (*right*). *Pierced Planes*, cherry wood sculpture, Dale Hallberg. Photo by Arlie Toulouse.

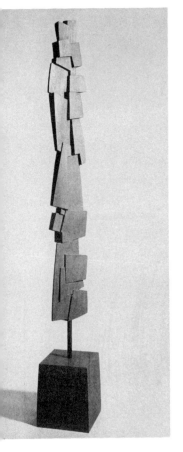

8 The art of group-doing

When two or more people join forces in creative activity, the satisfaction is multiplied by more than the number of participants. A man and his wife build their house together, and the structure becomes a symbol of their own growth. Our own home has taken seven years of spare-time work. We quarried the stone for the fireplace and have more than a fireplace; we have memories of the warm sun on the mountain side where we dislodged the rock, of the blue shadows in the valley when the truck was loaded at the end of day, of the sweep of wind that bathed our faces as we started home. All of these things now seem part of the structure. Our own thoughts and strength and work-play are the basic materials of which the house is built and are as real to us as the redwood and stone and glass and tile.

Children are fortunate who learn early that the elements of design are as much a language as the spoken word. Barbara Dean's children will never question this because they have experienced it. During a trip to Los Angeles they commented on what they saw—the lacing of freeways, the tall buildings, the foreign cars that had the shape of beetles, the television aerials, the whiz-whiz motion of many people and automobiles close together. Back home, they expressed the trip in line language, each of them working independently and then comparing statements. This is quite a different matter from a mother saying to her children, "Why don't you draw what you saw today?" Barbara also worked intently, the children caught from her the spirit of concentration and communication.

Helen Worrall, who teaches art at the Reading, Ohio, High School, has led her students through many group experiments in creative activity. They have laminated clear glass, placing various coloring agents between the layers and kiln-firing the stacked layers. More recently they have used crushed colored glass combined with liquid plastic on top of base sheets of plaster, first outlining their designs with metal strips of silver or aluminum. They have done a permanent installation of glass paneling designed by a senior student and Rosalyn Miller. *Every student* in Miss Worrall's class that year had a part in the doing. Funds to pay for the materials were raised by the student body as a whole. The method used was that described by Peter Ostuni in *Craft Horizons*.[7] The finished panel was fourteen inches by fifty.

Here we have a combination of community support (the student body), participation by a large group, and research into craft literature! There is high hope for the place of art in the everyday lives of Americans when inspired teachers like Miss Worrall lead high-school students in this kind of group creativity! They used an ancient technique to make their stained glass panel—a cloisonné or *plique-a-jour* process—but introduced modern innovations. Thus the art of the past and the path to art in the future are the intangibles fused into doing.

From Milwaukee comes the story of the group doing of the Boucher family. This *Milwaukee Journal* photograph, Fig. 107, tells us that here

[7] Peter Ostuni, "A New Technique in Stained Glass," *Craft Horizons,* April, 1954.

Fig. 104. *City*, India ink, Barbara Dean. Photo by Arlie Toulouse.

Fig. 105. *City*, crayola, Mark Dean, age 8. Photo by Arlie Toulouse.

Fig. 106. *City*, crayola, Debbie Dean, age 5. Photo by Arlie Toulouse.

FIG. 107. *The Boucher Family,* Milwaukee *Journal* Photo.

are three people completely absorbed, completely alive in the moment of doing.

Whenever one works in joy, the product, whatever the materials used, will be sheer joy (Fig. 108).

Fig. 108.   Donna Read with her Mosaic, *Iowa Wind-mills.* Photo by Lee Payne.

III *The art of choosing and arranging*

9 The art of choosing

It is freedom to choose which has given beauty its transcendency through the ages, often lifting us above futile controversies about the arts.

Enjoyment of the arts is often spoiled by those who insist that we like what they like. We may wish that others could feel as we do in the contemplation of something that is beautiful to us; but the only wish that cannot fail is that someone shall find somewhere, an object which will evoke in him a response of the same high quality as the object of our choice invokes in us.[1]

Allen Eaton

ESCAPE FROM THE ORDINARY

Everyone lives somewhere and that somewhere becomes individualized as soon as personal possessions are placed about. Even a strange hotel

[1] Allen Eaton, *Beauty for the Sighted and the Blind*, New York, St. Martin's Press, 1959.

FIG. 109. *Mermaid*, mahogany carving, Ramona Douglas. Photo by Arlie Toulouse.

room becomes a decidedly different place after one has opened a suitcase and taken out a traveling clock, a pair of slippers, and a robe. These three items, and what is done with them, reveal a lot about the owner of the suitcase. What kind of a robe is it? What color? Tailored or frilly? Is it precisely placed, casually draped, or thrown any-which-way across the arm of a chair? What perfume comes from it? Faint? Heady? Lavenderish? Where are the slippers? How are they placed? Heels together, right slipper on the right, left on the left? Are the toes bent under? Does one slipper lie across the other? Is the clock compact and simple or ornate? Is it wound or run down?

Let's pretend a set of answers, any set. Doesn't a fairly clear picture of the owner start to emerge? Now let's imagine *you* in the strange hotel room. Picture your robe, your slippers, your clock (or watch), and the manner in which you would disperse these objects. What do the answers tell you about yourself? I have just stopped writing to play the game with myself. My watch is not wound, and I probably would be quite amazed if I knew what time it really is. As I think about this, I know that it is no happenstance that my watch has run down. This tells me something about myself even though it does not tell me the time.

If only three personal possessions can reveal a portrait likeness, how much more do the dozens or perhaps hundreds of items we own reveal us to the world? Some of these may have been gifts or inheritances, but for the most part we have chosen them and arranged them. Each thing we own is a symbol of ourself. If the mail carrier should happen to notice which magazines he delivers to a certain box, it is quite likely he could make a fair estimate of an individual just from that knowledge. We stand truly revealed by what we choose. Creative choosing, then, must begin with self-knowledge.

We have all seen rows of almost identical houses set on almost identical streets. If we drive along one of those streets at night, some of the blinds will not be drawn, and we get brief glimpses of the interiors. These seem almost as much alike as the tract exteriors, and they blur together in an impression of dreary sameness. What do these almost interchangeable interiors reveal of the inhabitants? One has to conclude either that the people are as stereotyped as their quarters or that they are too timid to express what individuality they do possess.

I think that in most cases the fear of being different or strange drives people to seek security in what is ordinary. The commonplace is always safely inconspicuous.

One must not be too respectful toward art. Over-awe can intimidate one, with the result that creative production or choosing is impossible. Personalizing one's house with what one makes or buys should be joyous and amusing. Those who fuss their furnishings into congregation won't have any fun living with them. They will fuss back.

In almost every community in the land there are a few excellent craftsmen doing good things for the fun of doing them, perhaps without thought of sales. Seek out your local potters and blacksmiths and cabinet makers and weavers and mosaicists and painters. If you don't feel up to making your own creations, choose products from their skills that seem to you what you would like to make, had you the courage to try. If you spend sufficient time with these craftsmen you may find yourself gathering up enough courage to make the try! You will find a glow in these people. They are alive because they do not damn up the urge to form.

The mermaid shown in Fig. 109 was carved by Mrs. Ramona Douglas for her home in Corona del Mar, California. The mahogany panel over her front door is an architectural feature in keeping with the place and the spirit of a delightfully casual house beside the sea.

In the Pennsylvania Dutch country it is the barns rather than the houses to which decorative accents have been added. One of the delights of driving through that region is seeing the great red barns with colorful patterns beautifully spaced.

Alfred North Whitehead had a wonderful phrase to describe individuals who range in spirit and adventure with the mind. He called them *the vivid people.*

A vivid person is the opposite of timid. If timidity dampens you down and keeps you from making creative choices, it probably is because you mistrust your own taste. Vivid, we should point out, does not mean gaudy or gay to the point of extravagance. It means having the appearance of vigorous life or freshness, being animated, clear, spirited. Let us talk about this kind of taste.

THE FOUNDATIONS OF TASTE

Taste is an elusive quality which has to do with the solid virtues of sincerity and honesty and respect for the innate nature of materials.

It is possible to sieve clay through a strainer in order to shower the neck of a pottery poodle with a ruff, but violence has been done to the clay. The poodle may come out of the kiln looking ready to bark, but all that we see is a shallow triumph of manipulation. Those who admire him, and there will be many, most probably will use the word "cute" in their exclamations. The "cute" soon palls. Any delight in cuteness is fleeting.

When clay is fashioned into the form of a wild rose or the petals of a daisy or into lace, considerable cunning may have gone into the process. But there is a delicate difference between cunning and craft. When craftsmanship is dedicated to the artifices of cunning, taste is downgraded. We feel the fraud. Shakespeare must have been sensitive to the spurious in art and in life when he wrote:

> . . . *artificial strife lives in these touches, livelier than life.*

Let us now consider a decorative object of a different order (Fig. 110). The artist is Adolf Odorfer, one of our most accomplished ceramists. What do we see and feel when we contemplate this work?

First of all we know that a bird is represented, though we are not sure exactly what kind of bird. The form seems to incorporate the grace, the alert watchfulness, the just-alighted poise of all birds. We respond to the rudder aspect of the tail. Our eye follows easily the bounding edge of the form, delighting in the subtle variety and rhythmic quality of the curves. If we are responsive to beautiful line, we may have an urge to close our eyes and to resee with memory's eye the exact sweep of the curves. They are elusive in their subtlety so we look again, enjoying the second contemplation even more than the first. We may want to pick up a pencil and try drawing similar curved lines. We soon discover that although the form seems extremely simple, it is not easy to duplicate. Perhaps, like the best in writing, this bird-statement in clay seems simple because of its quiet confidence that actually comes from mastery. We become excited by the difficulties in what, at first glance, did not seem difficult. This bird is not so easily understood after all. Had he been a lesser artist, the man who modeled it might not have dared do without fuss and feathers. Because he knows beautiful form he does not need to dazzle with superficial aspects or to distract with contrived surface novelties.

We now want to get up out of the chair and walk around the bird, seeing it from all angles. We want to hold it in our hands in order to know the form through touch as well as through sight. The glaze is a dull matte green muted by the reddish clay beneath. It is good to look at and pleasant to feel.

We place the bird back on the table after having experienced it in all

Fig. 110. *Bird*, modeled clay, Adolf Odorfer. Photo by Arlie Toulouse.

of these ways. We know that we have learned more, both about birds and about beauty, from this bird form than we could have from any naturalistic model complete with detailed feathers and beak.

You have now given both our imaginary ruffed poodle and the sculptural bird in the photograph your thoughtful attention. Each object has elicited from you an emotional response as well as a conscious judgment. You should not prefer one object to the other because someone else does. You should listen to the reasons for his preference, judging them with your own reason and emotions. I sincerely want you to find the poodle cloying and to find the process used a cheapening of clay. I sincerely want you to find growing enjoyment in the bird. But I do not want you to hold these opinions because they are mine. If they can not be honestly yours, it is better for you not to agree. The first attribute of taste is personal honesty. If you like something because you think you should and not because you truly do, you will never develop a true taste.

On the other hand, one's opinions should be considered opinions and informed opinions, not the snap judgments of a closed mind. Opinions should arise from inner convictions. A conviction is quite different from a prejudice.

The art of past ages and of all the countries of the world is available to us now through photography, and we have what André Malraux calls our "museum without walls." Importers bring the craft products of all nations almost to our front door. *We owe it to ourselves* to be willing to look at strange forms and to give them our consideration. We deprive ourselves when we constantly retreat to the security of what is familiar. The adventurous spirit reaches out in an effort to comprehend.

There needs to be a spirit of brotherhood among those who project imagination into form. We owe this brother-in-doing the respect of sympathetic attention. What was he trying to communicate? If I don't understand, is the trouble in me? I will look a little longer with the mind as wide open as the eyes. It may be that we think we like certain things simply because we have never really looked at other and different things.

Taste is not something one achieves, like one's adult physical height, and then settles down to live with as an accomplished fact. It is an ever-growing process. Taste has nothing to do with passing fads or the colors some merchandising campaign has made the "style" of the season. It

Fig. 111. Wrought Iron Kettle, anonymous craftsman. Photo by Arlie Toulouse.

has much less to do than is commonly supposed with styles which have been sustained long enough to have become "periods." Taste does have to do with the ability to see the relatedness within objects and between objects and to assemble them with this in mind.

Elizabeth Gordon, the editor of *House Beautiful,* has taken the leadership in pointing out the difference between *style* and *a style*. "I'm modern," says one. "I'm traditional," says another. And the pointless argument is on. It is quite likely that the people using the terms do not know what they are talking about. Which modern? Which tradition? One contemporary object may have more in common with an article produced in the eighteenth century than it does with many other objects just off the assembly line.

For instance, we have in Fig. 111 a photograph of an old iron tea-kettle. We don't know how old it is. We do know that it went in a covered wagon to Montana with the grandmother of the present owner and that this was in the days of Indian ambush and frontier hardship. It is valued for these associations but its aesthetic value lies in its simple lines, its uncluttered contour, the charcoal color of the old metal which has been many times in the wood smoke of a campfire. It seems exactly right as a decorative accessory—a container for matches—in the contemporary home of the present owner, where the only war-whoops about are from small grandchildren playing at being redskins.

It is neither the date of manufacture nor the time of invention that determines whether a form is suitable in a certain setting, but the way it is related to the other things in the room and to the people whose room it is.

Sets and suites of furnishings contribute to monotony. Each item of furniture deserves to be selected for its own aesthetic worth and practical purpose, *to be something in its own right.* To furnish in this manner is to furnish creatively. One must be sensitive to each piece as an entity and as a part of the whole. This ability, as we have seen in the section on the Arts of Making, is the ability to compose, to make a *composition.* Without composition, a room or a design is hodge-podge and chaos.

Those who observe taste trends in the United States accuse us of three sins: first, timid and hackneyed choices; second, indulging in ostentatious domestic display in order to prove status; third, submitting entirely to "guided selections," by which is meant a thoughtless yielding to advertisements or to the preferences of an interior decorator who is given free reign to furnish.

The causes of these three faults are easily stated, but correcting them is not simple because they have deep roots in our economic and social patterns.

Timidity is an unwillingness to venture. It is a form of fear, and must be faced in ourselves for the unhealthy thing it is. Anything we do not understand inspires us with a fearsome awe and communicates a sense of mystery. An African tribesman does not like to sleep in the jungle. He will continue walking all night in order to reach a village. He is not afraid of attacks from wild animals but of the powerful spirits that are thought to inhabit the high bush. He *understands* animals so he does not fear them. I was willing to walk all night myself, but for a different reason: I was not sure that our campfire would stand off the jungle creatures. When we discussed our fears, it seemed incredible to the carriers on trek with me that I should be nervous about something which didn't bother them in the least.

"A person can *know* what a leopard will do," they said, "but who can know how a spirit will thief a man's soul out of his mouth while he sleeps?''

So it goes in our lives everywhere. We fear that which we do not understand. If we are willing to adventure into the accumulated knowledge of the past and to explore what is currently being invented, we begin to get glimmerings of understanding; our overawe of art is replaced by some friendly understanding, and we have a great, good time in the process. Overcoming timidity in our tastes is then simply a bountiful by-product of a larger spiritual adventure. The excitement of this adventure is enormous. No one should deprive himself of having it. The understanding one gains from this adventure is like a great glowing bonfire which stands off the leopards of doubt and indecision and boredom.

The more we learn and understand, the less likely are we to commit the second and third sins against taste. One of the first things we are likely to learn is that there is often considerable disparity between cost and value. When we understand intrinsic value we don't have to "show off." We aren't concerned with impressing others. If we are in the process of becoming, we no longer have to *seem to be*.

One of the worst things that can be said about an interior is that it "looks decorated." This implies that it is impersonal. It may be chic and smart. It may have all the "right" things, and each object may be related to every other object in the best possible way, but nothing has been related to the inhabitants. In this case "Turtle has not built and patterned his own shell." He has found one ready-made that is approximately the right size and has moved in, trying to accommodate himself to the strangeness with as much fortitude as possible, perhaps assuring himself that the shell he shows to the world is waxier and fancier and larger than one which could have grown naturally. After all, he could not have chrome-trimmed it himself!

The good interior designer, like the good architect, tries to guide his client into choices which are as close as possible to those the client would have made himself had he the self-knowledge and the design-knowledge.

Personal taste, then, is a preference for that one of many excellencies which is most excellent for one's particular self. It grows from self-knowledge, from design-knowledge, from open-minded awareness, from keen perception, from practice in selection, and from personal honesty

Fig. 112. Basement Stairs, home of Edna O'Bryan, Ames, Iowa. Hand-screened wallpaper on right wall. Decorative tiles. Dry arrangement in pots at bottom of steps. Iowa State University Photo.

which will not tolerate dishonesty of material or intent. If everyone felt secure in his taste, every home in the land would be different, not for the sake of being different, but because each individual *is* different.

CREATIVE COLLECTING

Every human being and some animals collect things. Most people would collect or accumulate more than they do if they did not in these days move so often. When moving day comes, possessions are sorted, and, since one can seldom take everything, some discarding is done. It would be wise to discard more things more often. All furnishings, all tasks, all conversations are dead things unless they are enkindled by responsiveness. I must affirm everything I own and everything I do by some feeling toward it. I do not own anything, even if I have paid for it fully, unless its presence adds to the radiance of daily living. Artifacts are accumulations, not possessions, until we find some unique delight in them. Any decorative object is a worthless trinket unless I stand in some spiritual relationship to it. When I cease to see an object except as a familiar blur in an accustomed place, I can no longer give it house room. I must react toward what I possess or that possession is an excess and a hindrance and an affliction to the spirit.

Some people satisfy the collecting instinct by accumulating stamps or antiques or buttons or odd dishes or old cars or glass slippers. The list of what people collect would take an encyclopedia to catalogue. I see nothing wrong with collecting if you respond to and are enlarged by the thing you collect. I could not be enlarged by collecting glass slippers, but I would be the first to admit another's right to do it and the last to discourage him. I can recall when I collected dance programs!

What one treasures changes as one grows and expands. A beautiful object is beautiful not only because of what the senses report about it but because of what the mind makes of it.

Mr. Allen Eaton set out to make a collection of objects of wonder and beauty which people who are blind could enjoy through the sense of touch. He discovered that sighted people found much in it for themselves. In this collection there are tools and utensils and many things from nature, including shells. This seems to me one of the most wonderful collections anyone might make. There is the challenge of hunting

Fig. 113.   A *Shape, a Pattern, a Symbol, a Fish* . . .
Photo by Arlie Toulouse.

for the objects, the aesthetic thrill of adding them, one at a time, to a meaningful display, and the added pleasure of using one's sense of touch to evaluate what one finds. Haptic sense is happy sense.

What one knows about what one collects adds to the pleasure. I have a little collection of starfish. They are not objects to feel, but objects to see for their shape and pattern. I am intrigued by the dots—here concentrated, there scattered. But part of my pleasure comes from what I have learned about starfish as fish and starfish as shapes. I know how to make a five-pointed star with a compass and, I know about the predominance of the number five in natural growth (not among crystals but in living things).[2] I know that during the Middle Ages a five-pointed star was considered a potent enough charm to ward off the Devil. What I know about the proportions within pentagons and what I know of the five-pointed star as a symbol all contribute to the pleasure I receive from my starfish. This is a collection which has done something for me.

Starfish may not do anything for you but something else will, and in a similar way. That is what I mean by creative collecting.

[2] See Matila Ghyka, *The Geometry of Art and Life,* New York, Sheed and Ward, 1946.

10 The art of arranging

Arrangements give us pleasure when they are made with wit. The coordinating principle is that of analogue and metaphor. When we make an arrangement we are concerned with degrees of sameness and degrees of difference. If there is too much sameness, the arrangement is dull. If there is too much variety, there is no unity. We can start by making a simple arrangement of the kind shown in Fig. 114. Here we have three bottles—Swedish crystal decanters. They are made of the same kind of glass, they are similar in shape, they form a progression in size. These are their similarities. Their differences are their height, volume, and the levels and colors of the liquids they contain. Another difference between them, and the one that gives me the greatest pleasure, barely shows in the photograph; it is the difference in the reflections they pick up. The three make a nice little unit, pleasant to behold, but the arrangement isn't really a witty one. Why? Because we don't have to search for the analogies.

FIG. 114. *Bottle Arrangement.* Photo by Arlie Toulouse.

Fɪɢ. 115. *Mask Arrangement.* Photo by Arlie Toulouse.

Our masks seem to me a more exciting arrangement (Fig. 115). They have in common that they all are masks, are hand carved by African craftsmen, and are in dark wood. Yet each mask is distinct, not only because its features and expression are different but because its implications are different. I look at them every day and have not begun to finish my inventory of their differences.

We place an old stoneware jug on a coarse handwoven mat, and the likeness of rough textures is enough to unify them. We place a black-on-black Indian clay pot beside a stitchery in which there are streaks of charcoal yarn, and the one color held in common is likeness enough.

The fun of arranging is to try this and try that and see how each thing changes in the presence of another. You are then *experiencing* the arrangement. Let us hunt for the analogies in the bookcase arrangement shown in Fig. 116. The rectangle of the hanging repeats the rectangle of the mosaic door. The little wrought iron dog repeats the color of the pot. The flat basket repeats the color of the lamp base and the background color of the mosaic. The arrangement is orderly but casual; it does not seem contrived.

I had read of "variety in unity" and "repetition with variation," and I partially understood the implications of these phrases, but the full import of analogue came to me through poetry. An analogy is a relation of likeness between two things, consisting in the resemblance of certain, but not all, of their attributes. A metaphor suggests analogy. By feeling the power of metaphor in poetry, I came to see what analogy can do in art. This was a tremendously exciting discovery.

In 1956 a book was published which, it seemed to me, would alter the whole of art in the future: *The New Landscape in Art and Science,* by Gyorgy Kepes.[1] If I were going on a trip and could carry only one

[1] Gyorgy Kepes, *The New Landscape in Art and Science,* Chicago, Paul Theobald, 1956.

Fig. 116. Bookcase and Silk Screen Hanging, Donna Read. Photo by Lee Payne.

art book in my luggage, this would be that book. It contains an entire chapter on analogue and metaphor. You will be missing a great experience if you do not find this book and give yourself to it.

When we furnish a room, set a table, distribute articles in a dresser drawer, or place flowers in a vase we are making an arrangement. The composition of a painting is an arrangement on a flat surface. Architecture, gardens, or sculptures are arrangements in three-dimensional space. We make so many arrangements every day that we can not begin to discuss all of them and how to make them orderly and satisfying. However, if we talk about a few of them and you master these, everything else you arrange will be affected by what you have mastered.

When one arranges according to some ordering scheme, one is composing and the finished arrangement is a composition.

COMPOSITION

When one tries to "compose oneself" during an agitating experience, one attempts to order one's thoughts in order to achieve a degree of tranquility. One tries to avoid hysteria or chaos by setting ideas in the proper relationship to one another and to the total situation. In architecture, in home furnishings, in design of any kind, composition involves the same process and has the same purpose. One composes by placing or connecting different things according to a plan in order to make a satisfying whole which is something more than the sum of the parts. An analysis of paintings that have withstood the test of time will reveal that these works are organized according to some plan, some scheme of arrangement, and this scheme is the composition.

I think it was Georges Braque, that master of subtle color and evocative still lifes, who said that when a lemon is placed next to an orange, it ceases to be a lemon and becomes a fruit, as does the orange. This is a poetic statement of the intereffects among objects.

But where and how does one go about composing? Is it a matter of seizing the lemon and eventually adding the orange as a sort of experimental afterthought? Or is the lemon, so to speak, in the left hand while the right hand clutches the orange as part of a preconceived plan?

I believe that composition begins with the frame and that the frame

Fig. 117. *Asymmetrical Arrangement*, Professor Mabel Fisher's class, Iowa State University. Iowa State University Photo.

is decided upon by an act of the intelligence. In a home the "frame" is the house.

In order to be specific let us assume that we wish to make a stitchery or a mosaic to hang on a blank wall above a chest. We have to decide whether we want a vertical or a horizontal panel. In older days it would have been a horizontal one, centered above the chest, but today it is more likely to be a vertical hung to one side of center, balanced by grouped objects set on the other end of the chest, an asymmetrical balance. The color scheme of the room has already been established, but we have to decide how much of an accent we want the wall panel to be. We will probably pick up the colors of the room in any case, but with variety. The amateur will try to match "my turquoise" exactly, but the more experienced designer will know that subtle variations on a theme are more exciting than "matches."

We have begun with the frame, we have related it to the furniture beneath to achieve unity, we have decided upon the principle colors. We have now to choose the forms of the design and decide how they will be related to one another and to the frame. We may use one of the approaches to design presented earlier in the book or we may use one we have evolved for ourselves; but in any case we will have noticed by this time that a design is a composition in geometry, that human, animal, and plant forms are variations of the sphere, the cone, the cylinder.

ARCHITECTURE AS COMPOSITION IN SPACE

"Architecture is like a great hollowed-out sculpture which man enters and apprehends by moving about within it." Bruno Zevi.[2]

House planning is composing in space for daily living. A house is an enclosed place in which to move about and do whatever one does in daily living, a shelter where people *move in space*.

Different people want to do different things, and varied numbers of people, depending on the size of the family and their social habits, are going to be doing things within the walls of the house. It would seem intelligent to let the walls, the boundaries of space, fall into place as a result of bounding the anticipated activities. In older days the thought often was to establish the boundaries, big or small, and try to fit the activities of the household into what had been bounded.

Perhaps if I tell you the story of our own house and how we planned it, what worked and what might have been done better, it will give some idea of how one might go about thinking of planning a house. I am sure that our house would "fit" very few other families, but that is because each family *does* different things. That is why it is difficult to find a tract-type house which exactly "suits" the customer.

First, I will tell you why we built our house. For six years we lived in a small "ready-made" house with two bedrooms, seven hundred and fifty square feet in area. Although we did considerable entertaining, we had no dining room. One of the bedrooms had to be used as an office (ours is a home industry) so there was no place to sleep guests. We had a considerable collection of African carvings but no place to display them and no place to store them when they were not being displayed

[2] Bruno Zevi, *Architecture as Space,* New York, Horizon Press, 1957.

Our greatest loves among the things we collect are books. Even after covering all possible walls with book shelves, there was not room under the beds for the books left over from the shelves. This will give you some idea of how the space in this house failed to satisfy our human needs. Clearly something had to be done. A new house planned around our rather special business needs and our personal needs seemed the best solution. We reasoned that since we needed to be at home almost all of the time in order to attend to the long firing cycles of our kilns, we would build this new house ourselves in our spare time. We do not recommend that every family build their own house with their own hands. This takes patience, a willingness to wait for what one wants, and a love of making.

In planning our house we first listed all of the activities we would want to carry on within the space of the house. We read, we write, we sculpt, we do mosaics, we paint, we entertain, I sew, my husband does wood engraving and carpentry. Of course, we eat and sleep, too. This was part of our list.

The second step was the scribble stage. We sketched traffic patterns of the movements involved in the activities we had listed. I type while I cook. A prudent cook will look now and then at what is cooking, so it was simple to scribble a traffic pattern from kitchen to typewriter. Students sometimes drop in to consult with me about a design while my husband is engrossed in something else—a scribble from outside to the office which doesn't touch the living room. All of the many scribbles represented the *movements in space* which we anticipated making.

Our third step was to sketch in the walls, placing doors where the most scribbles indicated a need for them. We then built a scale model with a removable roof so we could actually visualize ourselves doing what we knew we would want to do. In this stage we saw that we had not provided enough storage, although we thought we had included a great deal.

Next, we made decisions about materials. Of all the wealth of good materials we selected these: redwood, stone, glass, unglazed vitrified tile.

We chose redwood because we like its deep purplish-brown color which darkens and richens with age. We wanted the rhythm of a vertical repeat in the siding, so we designed a groove pattern, taking into account the stock sizes of lumber. After we had hand-grooved a sample board and studied it for effect, we arranged for the lumber yard to mill all of the siding to our design. There is no feeling in the wall of one board ending and another beginning—just a continuous expanse of a forward plane and a recessed vertical, deepened by shadow.

We chose stone because we like its feeling of stability and permanence and think that it gives a very real sense of shelter. We wanted color in the rock but muted color without shine. Nothing in the building supply yards suited us so we set out to search the hills of southern California for the kind we had in mind. We found it in a national forest about sixty miles from home and discovered that we could get a permit to dig it from the Forestry Service. We rented a truck and found we could dig and bring home eight tons in one trip. We have used twenty-four tons of stone.

The stone fireplace we built runs the entire length of the living room and extends past the corner to make a windbreak and background for our tropical foliage. My husband's experiences in sculpture and in prospecting gave him an eye for the grain of the rock and the natural fracture lines which would yield to a blow from the rock hammer.

We would not suggest that everyone should quarry stone and build his own fireplace—this depends upon whether one has the energy and a great desire to do it.

We wanted glass, floor to ceiling, in every window where its use did not diminish privacy. We used wide overhangs to diminish glare. In our fortunate climate we are able to get the feeling of living with the weather even while indoors.

As may be guessed from our approach to planning our house—shaping it around the activities that would be carried on within—the bounding edge, the walls, are irregular. The house bulges where more space was needed and indents where less space was needed. The indents have been developed as patios or gardens which *visually* fill out the rectangle, thus alleviating the feeling of tension that results from compressions of a basically geometric form. We could bulge or indent at will, because we used a flat roof.

There were practical things we needed to know of which we had no knowledge, such as how far a certain size beam would span, which walls would carry the weight of the roof, and many other problems which would have appalled us without the help of our friend, Ted La Motte, then an architectural student who had built several fine houses of his own.

Fig. 118. Bathroom, Dendel Home. Photo by Lee Payne.

Now that our house is completed, after seven years of working on it in our spare time, we enjoy talking about how we feel about it and what we would do differently if we were building another. In this climate we would again select the same materials. The unglazed vitrified tile which we set in all the areas where our first traffic scribbles were made has been particularly satisfying. Several hundred persons go through our home every month during our Saturday open-house hours. The tile shows no wear from this traffic; it is quickly cleaned, it does not need wax, and it is skid-proof.

The two things both of us enjoy most are the fireplace and the feeling of the out-of-doors which we have inside the house. In the bathroom (Fig. 118) the bamboo behind the plastic privacy-screen throws a

Fig. 119. Stairway Garden, Home of Edna
O'Bryan, Iowa State University. Iowa State University Photo.

living, ever-changing pattern into view. In another house, we would, I think, bring the glass down to the top of the sunken tub and place the water fixtures at the other end of the tub.

In an existing house where the garden was not planned to be indoor-outdoor, the same effect can often be achieved, as Edna O'Bryan has done in her stair-well (Fig. 119).

FURNISHINGS AS COMPOSITION WITHIN SPACE

After the builder has bounded space with walls and divided space with rooms or partitions, we carry on the composition with the furnishings. Again the starting point, let us hope, will be the human needs which these furnishings will satisfy. We have seen that they can not yield even physical satisfaction if the proportions are bad or the arrangements unbalanced, because through empathy we feel these things *physically,* whether we are aware of it or not. And we have seen that a home can be "right" in all these regards and still have a *spiritual* lack if what is unique, even though dormant, in the individuals who will occupy the rooms is not expressed through the furnishings and arrangements. I can not quite imagine any man feeling at home in a living room he did not help plan. If the man's only interest in a room is to defend fiercely the one chair he considers "his," he has not a very big stake in his own home.

Neither can I imagine a man feeling at home in a living room dominated by frills and furbelows of feminine invention. A woman may think she has expressed herself by ruffling yards of material. This is a moot point we will not argue here, but I think even the woman would agree, if she stopped to think about it, that a ruffle is not what she would choose as a symbol of the man she married. And is not the living room his, too, and all the family's?

The most important aspect of interiors is the interior emotions of the human beings who are going to live in the rooms. What kind of person am I? Are you? The other members of your family?

In our case, we are people who love earth things, nature's appearances, the grains of wood and rocks. These materials indicated to us that we would use earth tones in our color scheme and rather coarse textures in the fabrics (coarse but not rough). We are not plush or satin

181

FIG. 120.   Book Wall, Dendel Home. Photo by Arlie Toulouse.

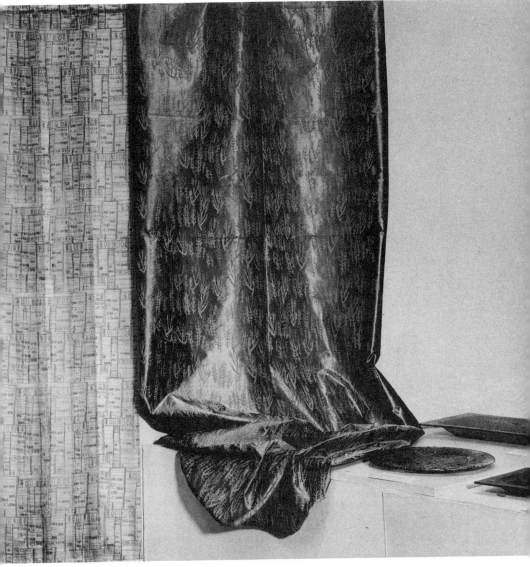

Fig. 121.   Spool Racks and Miniature Trees, silk screened fabrics, Janet Navin,
Iowa State University. Iowa State University Photo.

people, but that is not to say that elegance is not in order for other people and places. I am not suggesting any bias; only the opinion that "correct" furnishings for you are what reflect your own affections and interests.

Our biggest furnishing problem was the wall opposite our fireplace. We sensed that we would need something rather massive to "hold that end of the room down." Our solution was to build a long couch above which the book shelves would rise solidly to the drop-ceiling (Fig. 120).

It is great fun to furnish a home in these times because of the wealth of selection available. Never before have there been so many handsome materials on the market. Among them can be found drapery and upholstery fabrics which are suitable for the social atmosphere of a living room, materials which are elegant without enforcing the insidious domination of the utterly feminine. A woman can effectively express herself by making a good choice from among these. One of my students explained to me what she called "the ruffle psychology."

"When I was first married," she said, "I wanted everything to be real cozy. I felt so romantic that I thought of myself as floating on a pink cloud. I expressed this by ruffling up a pink cloud of gauze for the windows. When my husband, who is over six feet tall and a football player, came home and saw my surprise for him, his jaw dropped and after he had recovered from his first amazement he said just two words. He said, *'For me?'* Now I would be horrified at doing this even for *myself!*"

In Miss Janet Navin's silk-screened material (Fig. 121) we have an example of textiles so beautiful in themselves that it would be sacrilege to do more than the minimum of hanging and hemming.

Sculpture, like architecture and furnishing, is composition in space. In almost every community there is an art teacher or someone who sculpts and whose products may be purchased for a reasonable fee. More and more people are enjoying the thrill of owning an original painting or sculpture and of knowing the artist who did the work.

The happiest compositions result when the work is a collaboration of everyone concerned. In the fireplace wall shown in Fig. 122, there was united contribution from the owners of the house, Mr. and Mrs. Paul Elmquist, the architect, Mr. Burton Romberger, the decorator, Mr. Pat Oliver, and the designer of the panel, Mr. Jo Dendel. By consulting together they decided what color scheme would contribute unity, what

Fig. 122. Fireplace Wall Designed for Mr. and Mrs. Paul Elmquist by Jo Dendel. Photo by Arlie Toulouse.

Fig. 123. *Darned Burlap*, stitchery, Edna O'Bryan, Iowa State University. Iowa State University Photo.

material should be used, and what the general theme of the work should be. The material is unglazed vitrified tile which does not reflect any glare and which is available in soft, muted color.

COMPOSITION IN TWO DIMENSIONS

When an artist arranges on a flat surface of canvas or paper he is composing within the boundaries of a frame. As mentioned earlier a great deal can be learned about composition by tracing a painting by a great master. By shading the dark masses and leaving out details which might distract, one can see exactly how the darks and lights have been organ-

FIG. 124. *Serigraph*, Aileen Worthley. Photo
by Lee Payne.

ized. The coherence of the painting is a result of the way masses have
been organized.

Think of a weaving or a darning, and then try to make your darks
and lights weave. In our Fellowship we actually weave strips of dark
and light paper to get the feeling of "weavingness" when we handle
tones. We see that the eye can be guided through a composition in a
delightful way by total management.

Miss Edna O'Bryan's stitchery (Fig. 123) literally is a darning of
dark threads into lighter burlap. The sensitive placement of the darks
serves to lead us through the design area.

We are led in the same way through Aileen Worthley's serigraph
(Fig. 124). What is called the activity of shapes is, of course, the

activity of our own eyes moving among the shapes. Our gaze likes to be led.

THE ART OF MAKING A GARDEN

Henry David Thoreau held that a man is rich in proportion to the number of things he can do without. We might have an interesting midnight argument about Mr. Thoreau's statement, but we, at least, can not do without a garden. After listening to friends point out to us, quite reasonably, that we had no time whatever to care for a garden and that professional gardeners are expensive, we set out to plan a garden that we could take care of ourselves in a minimum of time. To relinquish the care to some one else would, we thought, cancel out one of the reasons for wanting a garden.

Different people want a garden for different reasons. Therefore before starting a garden I believe one should list what one wants. There are gardens for play, gardens for entertaining, gardens for quiet thought. The following is a list of our reasons for wanting a garden.

1. To have a wall for privacy
2. To have the pleasure of designing and building a beautiful wall
3. To add the purling sound of water to our evenings as well as the twitter of the birds and the ker-plunks of the toads who would be attracted by the water
4. To extend our living room by more than doubling its size visually
5. To give a proper setting to rocks we had collected on many camping trips to the desert
6. To watch green things grow and flowers unfold
7. To soften the hard edges of house and studio with the transitional grace of plants
8. To have a completely private place to meditate

The first service that a plant performs for you, whether it is growing or plucked, green or dried, is to soften the hard edges of things. Even before we had any plants growing we brought dry foliage in from the desert to soften some hard corners.

After the planning and the building of the garden the plants come next. You should not have more plants than you can enjoy. Enjoying a plant is a great deal more than just looking at it and having Words-

Fig. 125. *The First Service.* Photo by Lee Payne.

worthy thoughts about it although it is worthy to have Wordsworthy
thoughts. Few Westerners except Wordsworth have ever been able to
accomplish that. One's thoughts are more likely to be sentimental
thoughts. There is nothing wrong with that, I suppose, since so many
women get a pleasure and a brightness out of it. But I keep wondering
whether that road really leads to enjoying a plant the way a plant can
be enjoyed.

What is the difference between a Wordsworthy thought and a sentimental thought? You can get a hint of the answer if you read some of
the sticky nature poetry being written today. It is easy to find samples
in the magazines. You don't need to read much of it. Read Wordsworth
and Dylan Thomas later, saving the good for the last. In between read
Marianne Moore. If you can achieve her precise observation you are
on the right road. You are informing yourself about the plant, and you
are making original similes for its color and shape. Now what did
Wordsworth do beyond this? *He related it to human life.* He made a

symbol of the flower. He transformed the information which his senses relayed to him about the flower into something even greater than the flower. This transfiguration is what art is all about. What Wordsworth found in a flower was God. What Dylan Thomas found in the "green fuse" was energy. What you will find if you are capable of this may be something else. Who can be sure that these are not different names for the same thing?

We have said that there is more to enjoying a plant than looking at it and thinking whatever thoughts you are capable of thinking about it. If one isn't capable of thinking original thoughts about plants or if one just doesn't want to think at all, that is all right, too. One can just keep one's mind empty and open in reverence and the pattern and the rhythms of the growth forms will enter quietly of themselves without any fuss.

Sifting the soil through the fingers as you plant provides healing contact with earth. Watering and everything else you do to minister to a plant is something to enjoy. A flower is a celebration, and a harvest is a festival. If you have more growing things than you can enjoy in all of these ways, then the garden owns you, and all of these pleasant things become chores. Work is a chore when there is more of it than can be accomplished during the time available to do it. Limiting what you grow to what you can fully enjoy is one of the great secrets of having a successful garden. We have three *moari* iris. Each time one of them buds and blossoms, which is quite often, it is an event. If we had a great bed of them we would have a bank of color, but we could not delight in each separate blossom. Each one would not be a special thing. Hosts and multitudes make a different kind of pleasure.

One should try to experience the relationship of one plant to another. It would be worth a great deal of trouble on your part to locate the January, 1959, issue of *House Beautiful,* which shows in photographs combinations and creative manipulations of plant materials. We see, for example, ferns intermingled with agapantha leaves, and the article points out how they are alike and how they differ. (Identity and variety again, which is the basis of all arrangements.) After you have studied the photographs and thought about them, experienced them, you will know how to make your own combinations. You will be bringing Aristotle and Emerson and a new self (you) into the garden when you are able to make creative plant combinations. If you do not

FIG. 126.   Entry Garden, Gared Smith Home. Photo by Lee Payne.

Fig. 127. A Leaving Garden, Dendel Home. Photo by Lee Payne.

Fig. 128.   House into Garden, Dendel Home. Photo by Lee Payne.

know all the plant materials available and the plants' requirements of sun or shade or moisture, a good landscape architect can be of great help.

We have had interesting evenings discussing the kind of garden we would make if we lived in some part of the country quite unlike the place where we do live. Suppose we had the privilege of living in Tennessee near the Great Smoky mountains? In this location we decided it would be appropriate to have a roof line which brought into the living room the decline of the successive ridges of the five mountains we would hope to face. We would do as little as possible to the slope in front of the house. Would we then have no small, intimate garden? We concluded that this we would also need. It might be an atrium at the core of the house or a herb garden off the kitchen or both. We would need a little garden in addition to the great vista as our senses delight in the miniature, in those things small enough for all the senses to encompass.

Our own garden here in California turned out to be several gardens instead of just one. A guest enjoys entering a house through a garden and leaving through a garden, so first of all there is the entry garden. It is the introduction to the house. The entry of Architect Gared Smith's own home (Fig. 126) seems a promise and foretaste of the airiness and spaciousness of the interior. Also leaving a front door, the entry garden eases one from the color and light and shadow of a home into the hustle of the street.

Once one has arrived in the living room, one may pause there or go on to the garden. We tried to make the house extend into the garden by bringing the fireplace wall unbroken into the garden (Fig. 128).

Now on into the garden itself where we have enjoyed combining plants, rocks, and man-made objects (Fig. 129).

One of the great joys of a garden is the privacy it affords you. One recalls Emerson's suggestion of bending over and looking at the world through one's legs, head upside down, to get a fresh look at the familiar. I am hugely amused by wondering *where* Emerson practised this charming little eccentricity. I picture our frail, dignified philosopher surrounded by his illustrious neighbors in the days before high fences separated lots. I can imagine him watching the street and the houses next door for signs of temporary vacancy before daring to assume this

Fig. 129. Rocks, Plants, and Man-Made Objects, planting plan, Dale Hallberg. Lanterns by Donna Read (polyester and clay). Photo by Lee Payne.

rather odd posture. It was a comfort to me to think of a solution finally which may have come to him, too. He could have pretended to be weeding the vegetables.

The Japanese have known for centuries that a garden is one of the best of all places to meditate. If we import a stone lantern and model our planting after an Oriental garden, we have not achieved anything but the surface trappings of a Japanese garden. We have missed the great idea behind their gardens.

By a place to meditate, I mean a secluded area where the outer scene harmonizes with the inner scene of one's emotions. It needs to be a place where one can marinate in peace and let harmony penetrate, where one can regain completeness after the fragmenting demands of a busy day. There is no better place to renew one's vitality than in a garden, a place where things are vitally growing.

What then should grow in a garden? Climate is the first deciding factor. One of the reasons we like to live in California is that many of the plants we learned to know in Africa will also grow here. These are focal points of related memories. One of the functions of a good garden is that it is a place for joyous rememberings. The past is part of one's equipment for the present and the future. Poignancy is the spice of a garden. If you will read Marcel Proust on "A Cup of Tea" in *Swann's Way*,[3] you will know what I mean by that. I recall a frightened traveller on a ship Africa-bound just before the war. She was hugging a potted geranium every time I saw her on deck. I was too young then to understand why anyone would carry a scraggly geranium to a land of orchids. "It is all I can bring of home," she said.

Whether your garden is only a window box with chives or whether it is crowned and shaded by a noble tree, the roots of a garden can be what the Moslems call "the roots of heaven."

A MEAL IS A COMPOSED RITUAL

Setting a table is a composition that begins even before the choice of the linen, the silver, the china, the glassware. It begins with an *attitude toward eating,* a belief that a meal is a *ritual.* If food-intake were

[3] Marcel Proust, *Swann's Way,* New York, Random House, 1934, pp, 34–35.

FIG. 130.   A *Noble Tree* . . . , E. L. Reitz Garden. Photo by Lee Payne.

nothing but a zoological necessity, then the nutritionists could get on with the business of working out nutritive capsules, and we could have done with the whole business in one quick swallow. If a meal were not a ritual, cooking would be a monotonous, even intolerable bore. Any old thing would do for the table setting; the table would be nothing but the most convenient platform from which to grab food, and everyone assembled could bury himself in his favorite section of the newspaper while making blind stabs at whatever might have found its way to his plate. A person who reads while he eats is insulating and isolating himself from whoever else is present. By his act he is saying: "This print is more interesting than you are. Don't intrude on my first interest." He is profaning the ritual by ignoring its importance. Our fast-paced life has deprived us of so many small gracious rites that it becomes highly important to defend all that is meant by gathering at table and breaking bread together.

A hopeful sign is that men have started to interest themselves in what goes on in the kitchen and at the barbecue pit. They do not only wear chef's hats and silly aprons but actually take pride in the tools of food preparation—the sharp knife, the thermometer which indicates the interior temperature of the roast, the spit on which the meat turns. This interest is to the good and helps make the food ritual a joint affair.

Whether the meal is a picnic, a barbecue in the patio, or a dinner in the dining room, the accouterments of the presentation, the dishes and tools for eating, are as important as the food in transforming a necessary meal into a small, pleasant event. An event does not need to be a large production. The fare and setting may be extremely simple. What is important is the quality of thought that is brought to the assembly and the spirit of recognized contribution. The breadwinner has contributed the means to purchase. The cook has contributed the thought and energy to prepare and assemble. Those who have done neither of these can contribute with prompt and appreciative response, by offering the best of their thoughts to the conversation.

My steward boy in Africa referred to setting the table as "dressing" it and that is literally what he did. His idea of proper dress for the table included some imaginative manipulation of the napkins. He would make a starch of cassava paste, dip the linens in the paste, and iron them into fanciful folds suggestive of Japanese paper sculpture. My first impulse was to restrain him; but when I saw the pleasure he had from this activity I wisely let him do as he wished. In the course of time our habitual guests would rush to the table as soon as they entered the house to see his sculptures of the day done in spotless linen. We would tend to consider this elaboration a waste of time and in doubtful taste, but the boy's basic idea was right. He brought imagination and play to what might have been an onerous chore.

Once upon a time most families owned a "company set" of fine china. For everyday use they had whatever miscellany of crockery had been accumulated—undamaged remnants of former sets, odds and ends acquired as doubtful "dividends" for having purchased certain brands of cereal, the heterogeneous results of well-meant gifts. They also had sterling silver, which was brought out of its flannel swaddlings and vigorously polished for special dinners.

Now our ideas have changed. We have begun to realize that the formal dinner belongs to the day of inexpensive household help. We recognize that the time spent in keeping elaborate silver services polished might better be spent in taking the tarnish off our thinking by reading a stimulating book. We know that few of the houses being built now have adequate storage for several different sets of dishes. We know that few budgets can stand the strain of sterling.

It shows a bad sense of proportion for one to think that one can't start housekeeping lacking sterling and fine china and hand-blown leaded crystal. There are handsome patterns of stainless-steel tableware; there are exciting dishes in pottery and stoneware; there are good-looking glasses which are not crystal. Shopping for dishes which are similar in spirit, related, but different, in color, is much more exciting than settling on one matched set. If you do a good job of assembly, the result is a unity encompassing delightful variety. Dishes are the background for food; they provide the important negative shapes in the composition. A pork chop lying on a wild rose is disconcerting once one thinks about it. Women who select dishes with morning glories, wild roses, and tropical briars rampant across the surface just haven't thought about it.

Sir Herbert Read has been criticized by other critics for the important role he has assigned to pottery in the aesthetic scheme of things, but I find myself applauding his emphasis. This is not only because I happen to be a ceramist. In fact, my concern with clay did not just "happen." It grew out of my living in the tribal villages of Liberia. I was impressed with the Africans' pots, but even more with their attitude of respect and reverence for clay, the earth material with which they worked.

No one knows who first discovered that clay, baked to hardness, makes a durable utensil. Legend has it that baskets came before pottery and that daubed baskets were the first pots. An accident, perhaps—a reed basket set on the wet clay bank of a stream while a woman bathed and fished, unheedful of the falling sun. Then home late, the caveman husband grouchy with hunger, the hasty fire, the fish-basket carelessly close, the reeds catching fire and burning while the man gobbles the half-raw fish, the clay hardening as it fires. In the morning, incredulous neighbors standing around the cold embers of the fire, thumping the hard buff-colored object to hear it "clunk," saying how a miracle had been done, saying that mud has been turned to stone. And the man exhibits the first pottery any one in the world has ever seen, giving the impression that he has thought up this wondrous thing all by himself. The woman? She is down at the stream with a new basket, carefully impacting the reeds with clay to see whether the miracle can be repeated.

It may have been this woman's child or grandchild tagging along beside her who, having no basket to pack with clay, formed a little bowl without the reed framework, picking stones and twigs out of the wet mass as she worked, fashioning the first pot without a retaining form. Or perhaps this was many generations of grandchildren later. We do not know. But hundreds of generations of children since have shared what must be one of the most universal of racial memories—the urge to squeeze clay between the fingers and shape it into form.

Years must have passed. "The water is cold on the tongue," the man said as he wiped his hot face with a handful of leaves. Then he grabbed the water jug by the neck and drained the last good drop. The tribespeople no longer kept their water supply in gourds, for they had learned to coil the clay and wind it, coil on coil, until the jars were higher than any gourd they could grow. And they had learned that when water stood in the pots long enough to seep through the side, the wind cooled it, and it was pleasant to drink. The ware was harder now too, because they had learned that little ovens of mud were hotter than open cooking fires.

Just now I called the urge toward pottery a universal racial memory because the idea sprang up in all parts of the world among people who had no way of communicating with one another. But it was the Chinese who really did things with the idea. They tried adding this and that to the clay as they found it in a constant search for ways to refine and perfect their ware. It was they who first thought of adding bone— human bone from raided graves—to the clay. So well did they succeed that vitreous ceramics carries their name—chinaware. As long ago as two hundred years before the birth of Christ, the Chinese knew how to make glazes, and they made porous water jars from choice, not necessity.

When Chinese porcelain appeared in Europe about three hundred years ago, every effort was made to copy its perfection. Animal bones instead of human were used, and every secret of the craft was sought and tried. In our own country, in colonial times, the salt-glazed earthenware made here was considered crude and "everyday." All elegance and quality in ceramic ware must come from Europe, of course!

What then was left for contemporary potters to achieve after the perfection reached during hundreds of years of dedicated effort in Europe, after the great traditions of Wedgwood and Haviland had been established, after generations of women had learned to speak in tones of hushed reverence when mentioning "my bone china"? Most of the answer is in one word—color. Ceramic colors are minerals and most of them bleach out above nineteen hundred degrees of heat, some of them long before that. What was needed was a clay body which would give a durable ware when fired below the fade-range of these minerals. After a great deal of experimenting by men like Dr. Glen Lukens of the University of Southern California, a good talc base ware was developed. And so color came out of the kilns!

When most of the country began turning the last of the parlors into living rooms, others were moving their living rooms out-of-doors. The tone of life was set by sun and sand and surf, and it was informal happy living that called for the colorful and the casual in furnishings. These qualities could be had in pottery.

Colored dinnerware was not the only contribution that individual potters had to make to the nation's dinner tables. They started to think about form.

Why is a plate round? One reason is that a round dish can be made on a semimechanical device called a "jigger." However, much of the experimenting that was being done was carried on in garages or small workshops by individual potters most of whom could not have afforded the smallest part of the expensive equipment necessary for large-scale production. Since they could not take advantage of the economies of large-scale production, they were not limited by them—their only limitation was the extent of their imaginations. In some cases function may have been sacrificed to fancy, but at any rate experimental design began to function. Today the potters of the nation are among the most vital of our craftsmen.

Glaze is similar to glass in ingredients—it contains silica and lead and the pigments which give it color. Men have spent their lives developing unusual glazes and have said after years of work that they have only begun to learn. There is always the happy accident, the unexpected result, the excitement of opening the kiln with the experiments inside.

In high schools and adult education centers and in homes all over the nation, there are little kilns from which emerge wonderful products. This is particularly true in the New England States, in the Southern Highlands, and in California. In addition to these products there are exciting ceramics from all over the world from which to choose. Since that long-ago day when the woman went to the clay fishing-bank with her reed basket, the old miracle has been repeated many times with endless variation.

If there were space in this volume, we might go into the history of glassware and silver. These too have a wonderful past.

It is quite possible to select a good dinnerware pattern which is a suitable background for food and to find compatible glass and silver, without knowing that ceramics is one of the world's oldest crafts and that it goes back twenty thousand years. One can set a good table without knowing that magnificent colored tiles decorated the walls of Nebuchadnezzar's palace six hundred years before Christ was born or that the walls of Babylon were made of glazed bricks. But I think that it is more interesting to set a table if one *does* know these things. This kind of information is part of our inheritance, part of the wealth we possess because we live *now*. Sociologists are constantly pointing out

Fig. 131. Dining Unit, Janet Navin, Iowa State University.

Fig. 132. *Bantu*, Denwar. Photo by Herbert Bruce Cross.

that one of the troubles with present-day society is its feeling of being without roots. We have cultural roots going back into prehistory, but we are unattached to those roots and can draw no sustenance from them unless we acquire the knowledge that entitles us to our rightful inheritance.

Even in a small apartment food may be served with a certain flair that makes eating a ceremony. Miss Janet Navin designed and made her own dining storage unit on which an intimate dinner for two can be nicely served and graced with a flower (Fig. 131).

One responds to whatever kind of dinnerware one has. Ours is pottery so we like to set it on a textured mat. If we had china we would use a more delicate material (Fig. 132).

Stoneware is a high-fired ware similar to porcelain, except that iron and other minerals in the clays give it earth tones of color. It is more durable than pottery but has the same clay quality. Stoneware glazes are soft and lustrous in appearance but durable in usage.

Porcelain in simple, almost pristine shapes and excellent in quality is being produced in many countries of the world, notably in the Scandinavian ones. Tremendous effort is expended there in achieving form so beautiful that it needs no decoration. Whatever decoration is added is restrained and seems to emphasize the beautiful form instead of competing with it.

11 Judgments: how shall we know what we have wrought?

Judgments should be as creatively made as designs. We can not stretch out the art principles like a carpenter's tape to measure the worth of what has been done. If there were a tight, unvarying formula for gauging the beautiful, design would be a science, outside the realm of spirit and emotion. In using the art principles we need to assign them life values instead of considering them a sort of Procrustean bed on which every creation must fit.

When judging our work, I believe the first questions we should ask are: How much have we learned? How deeply have we felt? How much

205

happiness has been experienced? What pride of accomplishment do we feel? What we have created is a bit of life made visible in form. If the form was worried into being, it is certain to communicate worry. If it was done in joy, then joy has been given shape.

Each of the art principles has its counterpart in life and gains its validity from this life-source.

Unity, rhythm, balance, proportion, dominance—these are the life values we look for in art and call principles. They are not "just a set of rules" that someone made up in order to judge a work of art. As developments in photography enable us to probe into the nature of outer space, penetrate the inner structures of solids, and reveal the forms of microscopic life, the organization of the whole universe becomes more apparent. It is not the diversities which are amazing, it is the similarities. It is an almost religious experience to study the photographs in Gyorgy Kepes' *The New Landscape*.[1] Each of us is part of a vast order indeed, and this order is unity.

UNITY

It is not a particular wonder that the United States was able to produce a genius of the stature of Frank Lloyd Wright. The wonder is that an articulate genius was required to point out that the *natural* house was the desirable one!

I once saw a house plan which had been presented to a prospective owner for approval. The owner had studied it; he thought the room arrangement would do but was worried that the exterior was too plain. He had written on the margin, "Outside looks too ordinary. Chinese it or Dutch it up." As though character in design were something that could be cut out with a saw and glued or nailed on the surface! Unity —oneness—is achieved when each part is properly related to the whole. Confusion and chaos are the opposites of unity, and we cannot bear chaos in our lives, in our thoughts, or in our art.

Unity does not imply that every part of a composition must be similar. There can be much variety, but the parts must add up to a cohesive whole. You will know, I think, when you look at a design you have done whether it has unity. If your composition has one governing pur-

[1] Gyorgy Kepes, *The New Landscape*, Chicago, Paul Theobald and Co., 1956.

Fig. 133. Work and Study Center, Iowa State University. Iowa State University Photo.

Fig. 134. Relaxed Reading Center, Living Room of Edna O'Bryan, Mosaic Lamp by Edna O'Bryan. Iowa State University Photo.

FIG. 135. *Rhythm by Orderly Repetition and Related Sizes*, arrangement by Applied Art Staff, Iowa State University. Iowa State University Photo.

pose, that purpose will probably give unity to it. In the two photographs of Figs. 133 and 134 we know without any explanation what purpose was intended.

RHYTHM

Rhythm is a matter of intervals. These may be intervals of size, of color or tone gradation, or of direction. Forms and lines divide space into intervals just as a drum divides time into intervals. There is the sound, the pause, the expectation of the repeated sound. The sound may vary, the pause may vary, but an anticipation is set up which cannot be fulfilled except by repetition. One day will not be exactly like another day, but we have the day, we anticipate the night, and are reasonably sure that a similar day will repeat the present one in rhythmic sequence.

We may not be tuned to "the music of the spheres," but we have our own personal rhythms of work, of speech, of gesture. A freely drawn line is simply the visible record of a personal rhythm.

FIG. 136. *Rhythm by Repetition*, The Long Narrow Panel Repeats the Shape of the Door Opening. Mosaic by Edna O'Bryan, Iowa State University. Iowa State University Photo.

Rhythm can be expressed by progression of graduated sizes, by the curves of a freely flowing line, by orderly repetition, by radiation, by related movement. But these are dead techniques unless the rhythms they express are the rhythms of life.

We have been dominated by clock rhythm for so long that we have almost accepted this as natural. Clock rhythm is a necessary, unvarying, artificial device. Life-time is not clock-time. Our own individual life rhythms, our patterns of acceleration and repose, of action and rest, of doing and dreaming, are the rhythms we should strive to express in what we create.

BALANCE

Rhythm implies space-time relationships; balance implies weight relationships. A decorative arrangement or a design will communicate a sense of repose and equilibrium if both the things we feel as weights— the dark areas of a two-dimensional design, the forms of furniture— and the colors and values are balanced. This is arrived at not by a set of rules but by the empathic "feeling into" the arrangement. When the wheels of an automobile need to be balanced out, we know the jar and lack of ease of the ride. A lack of balance in furniture arrangement or in a design creates the same type of unease. We strive toward balance, not because it is an art principle but because it is a life principle.

The seesaw with the fat boy near the center and the small boy out at the far end of the plank is the classic example of asymmetrical balance. We consider this type of balance more interesting than formal balance where the same or very similar forms are grouped at an equal distance from the center. Asymmetrical balance is more intriguing because it is less obvious. We are wordlessly invited to participate in the arrangement by "weighing" the masses ourselves.

Fig. 137 is a movable construction made by David Vaughan. The stylized train moves along the track enabling the students to study the changes in design balance which occur as the train shifts positions. It is interesting to visualize the train in still other places on the track as one studies the photographs.

Mobiles are studies in balance of the asymmetrical type. Many people have had fun making them and have gained from this enterprise a

FIG. 137. *Construction for Balance Study*, David Vaughan, Orange Coast College. Photo by Arlie Toulouse.

decorative sculpture for their homes as well as a deeper understanding of the principle of balance. An inventive genius named Calder brought this art form to our attention. We would do well to study his work and to feel ourselves into the delicate balances he achieves.

PROPORTION

Proportion is the most commonly violated of the art principles, I think, particularly in home furnishings. Perhaps this is because the store display room in which we see an article is very different in size from the room in the home where the article will be placed. The size ratio of article to sales room is vastly different than the ratio of article to living room. We buy the chair or table or couch, have it delivered, set it in place, and discover that our room seems suddenly to have shrunk.

Or a housewife may see a room in one of the many home furnishings magazines and decide that the furniture is "just what she wants." She carefully notes the brand and the pattern name, rushes out to buy it, and discovers to her disappointment that it "doesn't look the same" in her house as it did in the magazine. She has not taken into account that in the magazine photograph the furniture was carefully scaled to the area in which it was set.

211

Strictly speaking, a ratio is the relationship between two measures, while a proportion has to do with three or more. A square is not an interesting shape in itself because no ratio is established. Both sides are alike, that is obvious; and there is no reason to have further concern with what is already fully comprehended. A rectangle whose sides are exactly twice its width is quite obvious too, so unless there is a good reason to use that ratio, we try for a more exciting one.

The ancient Greeks had some highly interesting ideas about proportion, and we can increase our own sensitivity to this art principle by knowing what those ideas were. The so-called Greek rules of proportion were not rules that the Greeks "made up." All they did was to formulate in words what they observed in nature, and keen observers they were.

"Why should I care about the rules of those old Greeks?" I once heard a man say. "I go out and study nature. That's my guide." He was much closer to those old Greeks than he knew. They not only went out and studied nature, they too were delightfully independent about arriving at their own conclusions!

We do not have space here to go deeply into all the interesting facets of the Greek ideas of proportion and to explain where in nature these proportions are found; however, we will explain how to draw two of their favorite ones.

The first is the Golden rectangle, sometimes called the Divine Proportion (Fig. 138). We start with a square and draw the diagonal of half of this square. With the length of this diagonal added to the half we started with, we have the length of a Golden rectangle. In arithmetic the ratio is 1:1.618.

The second rectangle is closely associated with the Golden rectangle and is called a Root Five rectangle (Fig. 139). Again we start with a square, called unity. The diagonal of half the square is used as a radius to draw a semicircle which establishes the length of the rectangle. It is obvious that here we have a square plus two minor sections of the Golden rectangle. In arithmetic the ratio is 1:2.236 (the square root of five).

I have measured American Indian rugs and African designs and have found over and over the Golden rectangle or one of the root rectangles. Now it is quite unlikely that any of the Greek observations found their way into the funded knowledge of either American Indians or tribal Africans. But they too have lived close to nature and have seen the manner of growth, the distribution of leaves on plants, and it seems quite likely that these proportions found their way subconsciously into minds which took pleasure in laying out a length that seemed right with a certain width.

When my husband built our fireplace, he had no conscious thought of making the opening in the ratio of a Root Five rectangle. He was simply trying to follow the instructions in a how-to-do-it book which suggested the proper-sized opening for the "best draw" of smoke. But the opening made by following the book was not pleasant. He took a chance on smoke by altering it until it looked right to him. A little more length, a little less height, then it "felt" as it should. Not until after the house was completed did we measure the opening and find that it was within a quarter of an inch of being a Root Five rectangle! (And the fireplace did not smoke.)

After one has used pleasant proportions for a while, there is no longer any need to measure them out. They "get into the hand" and become part of one's working equipment.

FIG. 138. *Golden Rectangle.*
Photo by Arlie Toulouse.

FIG. 139. *Root Five Rectangle.*
Photo by Arlie Toulouse.

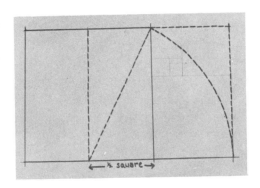

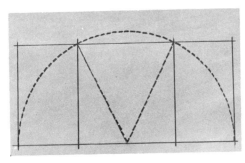

Fig. 140. *Disciples*, mosaic, Barbara Dean.

DOMINANCE

Just as every life needs a purpose or goal, every arrangement needs a dominant idea to which all other parts of the arrangement give support. In Barbara Dean's powerful mosaic, "The Disciples" (Fig. 140), the face which is the center of interest is central but not centered. Notice how the profiles of the other heads set up lines of direction moving toward the dominant head.

In Lee Hooper's design (Fig. 141) we again have a center of interest which is central but not centered. The emphasis in this design is not gained through largeness but through contrasted smallness, value change, and directional movement of line. Small though it is, the center of interest becomes important by being placed against a plain contrasting background.

In planning a room we need, I think, to consider what the dominant life activities in that room will be and to let our decisions of arrangement grow from these. In a living room we would hope that one of the dominant activities would be good conversation. This is a truly great art, and one that is in danger of being lost. One has only to read the *Dialogues of Alfred North Whitehead*,[2] recorded by Lucien Price, to realize

[2] *Dialogues of Alfred North Whitehead* as recorded by Lucien Price, originally published by Little, Brown, now available in paperback as a Mentor book, 1954.

FIG. 141. *Expectancy*, Lee Hooper. Photo by Arlie Toulouse.

what a delightful activity good talk can be. While reading the book one feels he is participating by listening. We may actually lay the book down for a moment and silently enter the dialogue. There is a reference, several of them in fact, to Plato. These references are likely to start us thinking. "I know a little about Plato. I know what he said about a shape being beautiful of itself. That was interesting, and this that I read here is interesting. I must find out more about Plato." In this way we join in talk with a man we have never seen and who now lives only in the thoughts that he left to the world.

Mr. Price gives us the setting for the conversations—the color of the walls, the way the books are placed, the name of the drapery material. These details are not presented as an inventory of furnishings—as sometimes seems to be the case with similar descriptions in Flaubert's *Madame Bovary*—but are given as a backdrop, an accessory to what went on, part of the *event* of an evening at the Whiteheads'.

In many homes watching television is a dominant activity, and the set exerts an arrogant tyranny over the room even when it is silent. The blind-eye stare of the empty screen becomes an *unwanted* emphasis. One method of solving this problem is shown in Fig. 142.

Just as a room can be dominated by a blank television set, one's life can be dominated by the unwanted. Our days can be dominated by details each small but insistent, and cumulatively massive.

Thoreau has a chapter in his *Walden* titled, "Where I Lived, and

What I Lived For." [3] It is a revealing personal entertainment to take Thoreau's title and try writing your own chapter. We tried this as a way of deciding what we wanted to be dominant in our lives. After this exercise it was easier to clear some of the clutter. What we wrote was quite different from what Mr. Thoreau wrote, though there were similarities, too. We do not want to simplify our living as much as he did; we do not want to discover our own version of a Walden retreat and go there to live. But we have tried to evoke the spirit of Walden in the home we have built and to capture what he called "the bloom of the present moment."

What you write for yourself will differ both from Mr. Thoreau and from us. That is as it should be. The important thing is to ask the question and to give yourself some good answers.

A pattern for living is so like a design or a room arrangement that practice in either carries over into the other. That is why art principles are life principles and not a set of rules to follow blindly or to resent, and why their interpretation is flexible and admits of wide latitude.

[3] Henry David Thoreau, *Walden and Other Writings,* New York, The Modern Library, 1950.

F<small>IG.</small> 142. Television Cabinet Designed and Built by Jo Dendel for
Mrs. Nell Parker. Mosaic Storage Doors by Mrs. Parker. Photo by
Arlie Toulouse.

12 Conclusion: Easter egg hunt in Serendip

Serendipity is the art of finding agreeable or valuable things which are not directly sought. I have loved that word ever since I discovered that Walpole had coined it for a tale which he called "The Three Princes of Serendip." I was delighted to find it recently in an article on *science* by Vincent J. Shaefer, the man who seeded a cloud with dry ice, causing rain to fall. The article, entitled "The Boy Who Learned to Grow Salt,"[1] tells how Steve Caldwell, while conducting research under the direction of Mr. Shaefer, discovered a new way to grow long fibers of sodium chloride. What he was trying to do at the time was something else; he stumbled across one valuable thing while looking for another.

Webster's second edition of the *New International Dictionary* defines serendipity as a gift. It is not for me to defy Webster, but I believe that

[1] *Saturday Review of Literature,* Dec. 12, 1959.

if this is a gift, it is one in the same way that health and many other good things of life are gifts. We may have been "given" them in varying degrees, but we have to look after these gifts, minister to them, or they fade away.

Serendipity is a by-product, just as happiness is a by-product, of what one does and thinks. Flexibility enables one to see and to seize on the chance happening—the unexpected, and flexibility is an attribute of the creative mind.

How much we lose of life because we persist in driving toward a goal with too great thrust! We refuse to derail from some fixed purpose. We refuse to condone the detours that slow down what we consider efficient.

Ozenfant describes, in *Foundations of Modern Art*,[2] how he experienced the famous caves of Les Elysies, one of the most deeply moving events of his life. He went there because his car happened to break down in the Dordogne. Fortunately.

Fortunately? It is fortunate only if one has the wit to experience what would otherwise have remained lost by being unknown. Therein lies the *gift* of serendipity.

Each of us can recall experiences when an unsought by-product became a valuable end-product. My husband and I once thought we might become wealthy quickly by discovering uranium. We studied diligently and prospected in hardy fashion. We did not discover uranium, not much anyway, but we became wealthy in a different way. As a by-product of our study of geology, we developed an avid interest in fossils and other formations. The wealth we acquired is the endless pleasure we have in hunting and collecting specimens of rock. The treasure we find in Serendip is not the treasure we directly seek.

Art is in the Kingdom of Serendip. How does one travel there? What passport is required for entry? Who are the people we will meet there? Who are the Princes of our time who preside over the kingdom?

Nothing as mundane as a road map will lead one to Serendip. Sharper seeing and more concentrated employment of all the senses than is habitual is the way to find Serendip. When all the alerted senses have made report to you, then you have to correlate these sense-reports and find the relationships that give form and meaning to what the senses have reported. This was what Emerson tried to tell us in many ways.

2 Amédée Ozenfant, *Foundations of Modern Art,* New York, Dover Publications, 1952.

I learned quite a lot about sharper seeing from my porters in Africa. They could see an antelope where I could see nothing but mottled shade.

"When you want to see a certain thing," my headman told me, "you look at everything real sharp, everything you see. Then you look again, slow-slow, for the one small thing that is different. That is how you will see game."

Emerson would have loved that headman. He knew how to find the different in the similar.

I also learned quite a lot in Africa about the similarities which exist between the apparently different, and that is important if one would get into the delightful kingdom of art. I had a volume of Emerson with me, and I read it until the covers were dog-eared and the pages were coming loose from the bindings. The cockroaches finally devoured what was left of Emerson. People said, "What a shame! The cockroaches have eaten that nice leather-bound book." I did not think it too much of a shame because by that time I had most of the words of Emerson in my mind. I did not have an understanding of many of the words as yet, but I had the hoarded words, so I could let the book go. The time when the words took on meaning was when I thought about them in the darkness of a mud hut. I began to understand a little about the perception of differences in what appears similar and the perception of likeness in what appears unlike. I began to comprehend the significance of metaphor and analogue, which is the stuff of poetry and of art.

Everyone who seeks to learn these things finds his own way to learn them. The search is quite a lot like an Easter egg hunt when you have to look under a great many flowerpots and bushes to find the egg. In Serendip the egg doesn't always look like an egg, so finding it requires keen perception. The salt crystals Steve Caldwell found growing were not the egg he was hunting.

If you are searching in science, people will be interested in your hunt and will let you look where you will. They believe in hunting for scientific eggs. But if you are looking for meaning in daily living and in art, some people will think you are wasting your time. "What is it?" "What is it good for?" "What is it worth?" Those are some of the questions people will ask who are just standing around and not hunting for anything themselves. And there are a good many people standing around, standing still and empty, who are not looking for anything.

Index

Page numbers in italic represent illustrations.

Affluent Society, The, 19
African wood carving, *17*
Analogy, 173
Architectonic design, 92
Architecture, as composition in space, 176–181

Balance, 27, 210–211
Berlin work, 20
Binary colors, 141
Blake, William, 73–74
Bleach print, *32,* 34–35
Blockprint, *113*
Bone china, 201
Braque, Georges, 174
Brayer, use of in direct print and rubbing, 38–39, *41*
Buber, Martin, 66

Carving, *71*
Cézanne, 144, 145
Chroma (intensity), 141
Cloisonné, 149
Collage, 48, *49,* 50, 51, *53, 72*

Color Areas, Law of, 143
Color balance, 143
Color scheme, 142, 143
Color terminology, *see* Design, plastic elements of
Color wheel, 141
Colors, cool, 141
warm, 142
Compass, subjective use of, 57–60
Compass doodles, 58, 60
Complementary colors, 141
Composition, 164, 174–176
in two dimensions, 186–188
Composition within space, furnishings as, 181–186
Crayola, *151*
Crayons, use of, in rubbing, 37
Crazing, 96
Creative collecting, 166–169

Darned netting, *92*
Design, dark corner to dark corner approach, 99–102
intuitive approach to, 73–81

Design (*Continued*)
plastic elements of, 114–147; color, 139–144; color terminology, 141; forms, 126–130; lines, 120–126; points (dots), 114–120; space, 144–147; texture, 130–139
subjective approach to, 45–48
through following structure of poetry forms, 102–104
through limitation, 108–112
with stick figures, 112–114
Dickinson, Emily, 76, 77
Direct print, *36, 37*
Divine Proportion, 212
Dominance, 214–216
Dots (points), *see* Design, plastic elements of

Eaton, Allen, 157
Emerson, Ralph Waldo, 194, 219–220
Empathic responses, 28–29
Empathy, defined, 21
Enamel, on copper, *97*
on silver, *116*
Enamel bowl, *106*
Enamel panel, *108*
Encaustic, 51–52, *53, 54, 55, 56, 57*

Fauves, 144
Feeling, defined, 29
Feeling and Form, 66
Fish print, 35
Forgotten Language, The, 76
Form, *see* Design, plastic elements of
Foundations of Modern Art, 219
Fractures, subdivisions of space, 94–99
Freud, Sigmund, 73, 74
Fruits of the Earth, 8
Furnishings, as composition within space, 181–186

Garden, art of making, 188–196
Glaze, 202
Glenn, John, 28
Golden, rectangle, 212, *213*
Graffito, *138,* 139
Greyed colors, 141
Guatemalan weaving, *109*

Haiku, 73–81
Henri, Robert, 75
Hopkins, Gerard Manley, 5
Hue, 141

Index of American Design, The, 20
India ink rubbing, *35*
Industrial Revolution, 18
Intensity (chroma), 141
Intuition, 74
Impasto, 56
Impressionists, 144

Jefferies, Richard, 28
"Josephine the Singer or the Mouse Folk," 6

Kandinsky, 99
Kepes, Gyorgy, 173, 206
Kits, commercial, 20
Klee, Paul, 112
Kostelanetz, André, 8

Last Judgment, The, 18
Lathe rooster, *72*
Law of Color Areas, 143
Laws of the universe, in art, 33
Leaf rubbing, *95*
Line, as design element, 25–27
over mass, 70–73
See also Design, plastic elements of
Linoleum blockprint, *98,* 118

Maritain, Jacques, 73, 76
Matisse, Henri, 8–9
May, Dr. Rollo, 74
Meal, as composed ritual, 196–204
Metaphor, 76
Mobiles, 211
Modeled clay, *116, 161*
Modern Prints and Drawings, 124
Monoprint, *125,* 126
Morris, William, 19
Mosaic, *59, 61, 89, 91, 98, 99, 100, 101, 107, 134, 138*
Munakata, 67–68
Munsell system, 140

Natural forms, awareness of, 33–40
Negative shapes, 61–62
Neutral colors, 141
New Landscape in Art and Science, The, 173

One-point perspective, 145
Ordinary, escape from the, 157–160

Perspective, one-point, 145
Planes, overlapping and interpenetrating, 146, *147*
Planting plan, *195*
Plato, quoted, 87
Plique-à-jour, 149
Poetry forms, and design, 102–104
Pointillists, 144
Points (dots), *see* Design, plastic elements of
Prang system, 140, 141
Primary colors, 141
Proportion, 211–213

Read, Sir Herbert, 17
Related colors, 141
Renaissance, 18
Repetition, with variation, 104–108, 173
Rhythm, 208–210
Roller, *see* Brayer
Root Five rectangle, 212, *213*
Rubbing, 37
    crayon rubbing, *38*
    leaf rubbing, *38*
Rulers, 87–94

Sandburg, Carl, 76
Scribbles, 62, *64, 65*
Scribble stitchery, *65*
Sculpture, 184
Secondary colors, 141
Serigraph, *187*
Shade, 141
Shakespeare, 160
Silk Cotton Tree, The, 47
Silk screen, *89, 122, 183*
Solitude, 74

Space, subdivisions of, 94–99
    See also, Design, plastic elements of
Spectrum colors, 141
Spirit drawings, 74
Stick figures, 112–114
Stitchery, *63, 90, 111, 186*

Taste, foundations of, 160–166
Tastemakers, The, 33
Tapestry, *107*
Tertiary colors, 141
Texture, *see* Design, plastic elements of
Thompson, Sir Wentworth D'Arcy, 78
Tempera paint, use of, in direct print, 35–36
Thomas, Dylan, 40
Thoreau, Henry David, 33, 188, 215–216
Tint, 141
Tool, leadings from the, 65–69

Unity, 144, 173, 206–208
Universe, laws of, in art, 33

Value, 141
Van Gogh, letters of, 133
Variety in unity, 173
Vaughan, David, 27
Verse structure in design, *104, 105*
Voss, Dr. Knud, 50

Walden, 215–216
Warm colors, 142
"When All My Five and Country Senses See," 40
Whitehead, Alfred North, 159–160, 214
Whitman, Walt, 28
Whittling, 69
Wordsworth, 189
Wood carving, African, *17*
Wood engraving, *136*

Yin-Yang, 85

Zevi, Bruno, 176

DATE DUE

MAR 4 '65	RESERVE	
JUN 21 '65		
DEC 17 '65		
FEB 10 '66	RESERVE	
JAN 18 '67		
MAY 24 '67		
JUL 12 '67		
FEB 17 1968	DEC 15 1979	
	SEP 23 1981	
APR 13 1969	APR 12 1982	
OCT 7 1969	APR 10 1986	
FEB 10 1970	MAY 21 1989	
FEB 24 1970	OCT 19 1996	
APR 8 1974		
RESERVE		
DEC 18 1975		
JAN 27 1976		
GAYLORD		PRINTED IN U.S.A.

N7430 .W34   c.1
Warner, Esther Sietm   100106 000
Art: an everyday e

3 3 0 00059389 5
GOSHEN COLLEGE-GOOD LIBRARY